GREATEST CRAPS GURU IN THE WORLD

"Not knowing why a particular side of an unloaded die turns up cannot make the act of throwing it, or of betting on it, immoral. If we consider games of chance immoral, then every pursuit of human industry is immoral; for there is not a single one that is not subject to chance, not one wherein you do not risk a loss for the chance of some gain."

- - Thomas Jefferson

Mark Jackson
David Medansky

Library of Congress Control Number: **2015909941**

Jackson, Mark
Medansky, David

I. Title 1. Craps. 2. Dice 3. Casino 4. Gambling.
II.   1. Art of War. 2. Sun Tzu 3. III. NFL

Editing by: Will Duffy

ISBN-13: 978-1512398410
ISBN-10:1512398411

Printed in the United States of America

10 9 8 7 6 5 4 3 2 1
First Edition

Greatest Craps Guru, LLC
greatestcrapsguru@gmail.com
www.greatestcrapsguru.com

"Be who you are and say what you feel because those who mind don't matter and those who matter don't mind." - - Dr. Seuss

[This page Intentionally Left Blank]

WHO THE HECK ARE MARK JACKSON AND DAVID MEDANSKY AND WHY SHOULD YOU READ THEIR BOOK?

Mark Jackson played in the NFL as a receiver for nine years. He was selected by the Denver Broncos in the sixth round of the 1986 NFL Draft as a wide receiver from Purdue University. (Go Boiler Makers!) Jackson spent nine seasons in the NFL from 1986 to 1994 for the Broncos, the New York Giants, and the Indianapolis Colts. He played in Super Bowls XXI, XXII and XXIV with the Broncos. It was Jackson who caught the touchdown pass from John Elway that sent the game into overtime on "The Drive" in the Broncos' January 11, 1987, AFC Championship Game victory over the Cleveland Browns. Along with Vance Johnson and Ricky Nattiel, Jackson comprised the "Three Amigos" receiving combination in the late 1980s. Undoubtedly the most colorful of the three, Mark Jackson possesses a smile that won't quit and a huge heart to go with it.

Mark learned the game of craps on a visit to Caesars Palace, Las Vegas. Much like any tourist, he learned to play the game from the dealers. Many years later, he spent two years as a Casino Credit Executive at the iconic Caesars Palace. It was then he learned what happens behind the scenes and the many secrets of the casino business. He embraced the old adage: "If you can't beat'em... join'em." He's taken those trade secrets along with his personal experience and he's sharing them with you in this book.

David Medansky is a world class authority on the game of craps, trusted advisor and published author of **Wholly Craps**; **Craps: A Winning Strategy; Craps: Playing for the Money;** and **Walk Away Craps**. Medansky has been playing craps for more than 20 years.

David has studied the game of craps and has played craps with premier professional craps players in Las Vegas and in the gaming industry, including, but not limited to, "Snake," "Little Joe," Beau Parker a/k/a "Dice Coach," Larry Edel, S.A. and Jerry Patterson, just to name a few. His students generally win eighty-five percent of the time when they apply David's principles and philosophies.

Even though this book is fiction, it may be the most important book you ever read about craps. This statement is made because what is advocated about playing craps in this book is considered to be *"radical"* by other authors, professional gamblers, and professional craps dealers. It differs from other books about craps in that it explores the mental, emotional and psychological aspects of the game. This book delves into the discipline necessary to consistently win at craps.

No doubt some of you have read other books about craps, attended workshops, seminars, courses and clinics that professed to teach you to win at playing craps. But what happened? The obvious answer is that you did not learn how to **consistently** win at craps. If you did, you most likely would not be reading this book. The information presented here will teach you how to think outside the box about the game of craps and you will learn various betting methodologies and philosophies of playing craps not found anywhere else.

In the many hours of playing craps we've found something very, very, very, very, very strange… It is that two people with similar strategies can be playing at the same table over the same period of time and at the end of the session, one walks away with a profit and the other is broke. Why?? Just think of all the knowledge it takes to play craps as a *bucket of water.* Both players have a full bucket. Both have *knowledge*; how to make bets, what the bets pay… both have all of the tools for success. What we've found, however, is if you have just a small hole in your bucket it makes a world of difference. That can be the difference between winning and losing.

You see we live in a world of duality. There's up and down, right and left, hot and cold. Just knowing how to make certain bets or what bets to make, the knowledge which we've labeled as the **OUTER-GAME** of craps, is not enough. We've discovered to make playing craps profitable you must understand the mental, emotional, and psychological aspects: **THE INNER-GAME** of craps. We've found, when people combine the **OUTER-GAME** with the **INNER-GAME,** virtually everyone walks away a WINNER! The objective of this book is not only to entertain you, but to teach you mental, emotional and psychological principles and concepts along with some various betting techniques. We hope that by your implementing what you learn from this book you will be a *consistent* winner at the craps table. Read and re-read this book. Study it until you can fully grasp and understand the ideas being set forth. This is the type of book you should not read just once and put away. Take notes!

We are asking you to trust the concepts and ideas set forth in the following pages. If you properly apply the principles, ideas and concepts in this book, the results will speak for themselves. Medansky's students have told him that they consistently win at the craps tables when they follow the rules, betting ideas and methodologies presented here. It is when they deviate from the principles advocated in this book and do not follow the rules that they lose money playing craps. Question: *Would you like to win or lose?*

Please forget everything you *know* about playing craps.

For those of you who have played the game and learned from other sources, you get to unlearn. Don't hold on to the *experience* that you have because if it were good, you wouldn't have this book in your hands. Read this book as if you're learning for the very first time. For those of you who have never played, you're incredibly lucky to have this book in your hands.

"It's not what you don't know that gets you into trouble; it's what you know for sure that just ain't so."

–Mark Twain

NOTE:

There are many clinics that teach how to influence dice at the craps table. The **ONLY** dice influencing course and craps clinic we endorse and recommend is taught by **Little Joe Craps**, www.littlejoecraps.com.

We also endorse and recommend Marty Seldin of **Club Vegas, Denver, Colorado,** www.casinoplayerjunkets.com for craps classes and other casino games.

Forward
By Martin Seldin

Having been anointed The Professor of Crapology by a noted Denver, Colorado sports journalist, I have taught many, many casino players how to play Craps.

Having spent more than 20 plus years in casinos from coast to coast, from domestic to international, as a Casino Junket Rep, I have observed countless people enter a casino with no more knowledge about casino gaming, it's theory and workings, then these are just "four (4) walls". They do nothing more than throw their hard earned $$$ away with no hope of winning, let alone at least being a competitive player.

As a component of my Craps class, a fair amount of time is spent discussing the essence of casino gaming as it applies to whatever casino game one is playing, be it machines, BJ, Craps, etc. Discussed is house percentage, bankroll, discipline, expected rate of return, planning, average bet v. bankroll size,…all easy concepts to understand, though as this book points out, very difficult to implement – it takes practice, perfect practice.

Invariably, somewhere in the course of my seven hour Craps class, someone will ask me to recommend a book to read about Craps. With the exception of **Wholly Craps!** by David Medansky, as of yet, I have not found a good, detailed enough book to recommend. That said, you are holding in your hands the **Greatest Craps Guru In The World**, a book that I can unequivocally say does one excellent job, in an entertaining story format, teaching the "how to" succeed at casino gaming as the principles described pertain to all casino games, not just Craps. Read this book, then re-read it again and again, digest and take to heart the principles of planning, setting limits, reasonable goals, what to do and what not to do at the tables and in the casino, and then, and only then can one start to learn their game of choice and become a competitive casino player at it.

There are more than fifty (50) different bets that can be made at the Craps table; so it stands to reason there are numerous ways to play, some good, most bad. I, like the authors, have stood at a Craps table, watched countless people play, wondering… "Where did they learn that?" True, many casinos will have a free "class" on how to play. They last about 45 minutes, compared to my class that is seven (7) hours. All they are teaching is how to make a few bets. Nonexistent are the whys and all the other bets, comparing the pros and cons of each. They do not teach you the reasons for betting, or not betting. True, the dealers will help a customer but he/she is busy working the table; the best they can teach is a few bets but not the whys or why not's.

I don't necessarily agree with the authors in their methodology or reasoning as to their approach to playing. Let us just say we have a healthy disagreement. But that's okay because one should always be listening and learning from others so that they can properly self re-evaluate. This is not to say theirs is bad and mine is good nor vice versa, just both credible, but different.

I stand firm in my belief that there is no substitute for going to a class taught by one of knowledge and getting ones "hands dirty" playing. However, if one can only read a book, one book, then with this book and its principles, one cannot go wrong.

Marty Seldin
Club Vegas, Denver, Colorado
Host of…the Safe Bet Radio Show

Introduction

This modern classic paints a vivid word picture of what it truly means to be the Greatest Craps Guru in the World.

Here is the story of a retired National Football League (NFL) player who becomes intrigued by the casino game of craps. He tries to use the principles and practices that made him successful in the league on this game and gets clobbered... To him, it's not about the money as much as it is about WINNING.

The game of craps was incredibly frustrating and expensive for him until he met the 'Greatest Craps Guru in the World'. Over the course of several weeks, his life was transformed as he absorbed lessons about business values, listening, patience, self-control, discipline, and more as it was applied to playing the game of craps.

Revealing the 'be' side of the business of playing craps that is often overshadowed by the 'do' side, this book is more than a technical how-to explanation... more than a feel-good story. It is a philosophical view of the perceptions of a professional craps player and the myths that surround the game.

A first-hand, inside look at the TRUTH about success in playing craps to make money, this book has the power to truly change your life.

If today's "wannabe" gambling entrepreneur could read only one book on the business aspect of the gaming industry, this book would have to be it - no other book shows so clearly what it means to be successful in the gaming industry.

Read it and truly KNOW what it feels like to be a professional craps player. Who is the Greatest Craps Guru in the World? **Read and learn...**

"An entrepreneur is the only person I know who can go from sheer terror to sheer exhilaration and back every 24 hours. You've got to have a strong mind and a strong heart to make things happen, and it will be a rough ride if you don't have both of these. Plus, it won't last long if you don't absolutely love what you're doing."

- - Dave Ramsey

"A craps player is the only person I know who can go from sheer exhilaration to sheer terror and back every few minutes. You've got to have a strong mind and a strong heart to be successful playing craps." - - David Medansky

Chapter ONE
A Chance Encounter

Similar to New York, Vegas is a city that never sleeps. The casinos are open seven days a week, fifty two weeks a year. Chris Rouser walked up to the craps table in Mandalay Bay, dropped down ten one hundred dollar bills on the layout; a total of one thousand dollars. The dealer pushed over several stacks of chips -four black, a stack of twenty greens and a stack of twenty red with black chips denoting one hundred dollars, green denoting twenty-five dollars and red denoting five dollars, "Good luck Mr. Rouser," the dealer said.

Chris stood next to Michael Caldwell. Caldwell was focused on the action at the table and paid no attention to Chris or his gregarious, good nature, and boisterous demeanor. A new shooter took two dice, threw them off the back wall of the craps table and established a point of Nine. Michael asked the dealer to place ten dollars on the Four, Nine and Ten, twenty-five on the Five and thirty each on the Six and Eight. Michael then placed a ten dollar Field bet. Michael's total bet was one hundred twenty-five dollars. Chris made a typical bet, twenty-five dollars on the Pass Line and backed it up with one hundred and twenty-five dollars full odds. He then made a Place bet on the Six and Eight for thirty dollars each; a total of two hundred and ten dollars.

Chris, a former NFL receiver, played nine years in the league and was fortunate enough to appear in three Super Bowls. The fact that his team lost all three Super Bowls sometimes haunted him. Subconsciously he could not shake the feeling of failure despite his numerous successes in life. His luck at the craps table had not been much better. Chris loved the game of craps. The excitement, the adrenaline flow, at times, could match that of a NFL game, but he could never consistently win. Today, however, Chris' life was about to change in a positive way.

The next roll of the dice was a Five. Michael was paid thirty-five dollars for his bet on the Five, but lost his Field bet, a net win of twenty-five dollars. Michael replaced his ten dollar Field bet.

Chris smiled at Michael as Michael picked up his winnings.

The next roll was a Four. Michael won eighteen dollars on the Four and ten dollars for his Field bet, a net win of twenty-eight dollars. He then asked the dealer to turn all his bets off. Chris looked at Michael thinking this guy was a nut case. He had never seen anyone turn their bets off.

The next roll of the dice was a Seven out; every person who bet on the Pass Line and took odds and made Place bets lost. Everyone at the table groaned as they all lost, except for Michael, who had turned his bets off. Chris, who lost more than one hundred dollars, noticed that the dealer did not collect Michael's bets. This perked his interest.

The next shooter rolled a Seven on the Come-out roll and the dealer called out, "Seven front line winner." Chris picked up his winnings from his Pass Line bet. He eyed Michael and saw that Michael did not make a Pass Line bet. "What the heck was this guy doing," he thought.

The shooter rolled the dice again; three and one showed on the top faces. The dealer called out, "Four, mark the Four." Chris started to make bets like a madman, "Dealer place the Six and Eight for thirty dollars each," as he put three green chips on the Come area. Chris then tossed the stick person four five dollar chips, "All the hard-ways," he said. He put another three green chips behind his Pass Line bet to take the odds.

Michael meanwhile, asked the dealer to "turn on" (or have

his bets working) for the same bet he had made previously. The shooter rolled a pair of three's, a Hard Six. "That's more like it," Chris called out. The dealer paid Chris Thirty-five dollars for his Place bet on the Six. The stick person instructed the dealer to pay Chris another forty-five dollars for his Hard Six wager.

Michael was paid thirty-five dollars for his Place bet on the Six. He then asked the dealer to take down his bets. Chris was a little annoyed that Michael wasn't going to be along for the ride. To him, Michael's taking his bets down showed a sign of disbelief that the roll would continue. He turned to face Michael, "Hey, what do you think you're doing? This guy is going to be hot. Do you really want to miss this roll?"

Michael said, "Good luck. I'm just taking my bets down."

Chris was visibly irritated and thought to himself, "This guy is scared and is trying to jinx the table."

Michael brought down his bets to protect his winnings.

Chris called out with enthusiasm, "Let's go shooter."

The shooter picked up the two dice and tossed them as Chris called out, "Come on shooter let's see a pair of twos – Hard Four."

The shooter tossed the dice as they flew across the green felt layout Chris and a few other players shouted out "Hard Four." The dice hit the back wall of the table, bounced around as if dancing on the felt before a four and three appeared.

"Seven out - line away, three and four means no more," the stick person called out. The dealers' hands moved quickly like a Hoover vacuum sweeping all of the players' chips away. The dealers sorted the chips by their color and placed them in stacks in the casino bank to be locked up.

Chris shook his head. He glared at Michael with disdain. Michael saw Chris glaring at him but dismissed it without a second thought.

The stick person passed five dice to the next shooter. The shooter picked up all five dice and rolled them backwards. He then picked the two dice that showed a four on the top face. The stick person used the stick to retrieve the three other dice and placed them in the dice bowl.

Chris made a twenty-five dollar Pass Line bet. The shooter rolled a three and five. The dealer called out "Easy Eight, Eight came easy, mark it."

Chris placed *five* twenty-five dollar green chips behind his Pass Line bet as odds. If the shooter rolled another eight before a seven, Chris would be paid twenty-five dollars for his Pass Line bet and one hundred fifty dollars for his one hundred twenty-five dollar behind the line odds bet. Chris placed two red five dollar chips and two green twenty-five dollar chips in the area marked "Come" and said to the dealer, "Place the Six." He then tossed another four five dollar chips to the stick person and said, "All of the hard-ways;" and placed twenty-five dollars in the area marked "Come" as a Come bet.

Michael watched Chris with curiosity as Chris made his bets. Michael made his usual bet of ten dollars on the Four, twenty-five dollars on the Five, thirty dollars on the Six and Eight each, ten dollars on the Nine and Ten; plus a ten dollar Field bet; a total combined bet of one hundred twenty-five dollars.

Michael's bet looked like this:

4	5	6	8	9	10	Field	
$10	$25	$30	$30	$10	$10	$10	= $125

Chris' bet looked like this:

6	Pass Line (8)	Odds on PL	Hard Ways	Come	
$60	$25	$125	$20	$25	= $255

The shooter rolled a five and one, easy Six. Chris said to the dealer, "Ok here we go."

Chris' Come bet went to the Six. The dealer asked Chris, "How much for odds, sir?" "Down with max odds," he replied. The dealer placed seventy dollars from his Place bet winnings plus fifty-five dollars from his sixty dollar Place bet as odds on the Six Come bet making it a total of one hundred fifty dollars. The dealer put a five dollar chip in front of Chris for his change. Chris placed another twenty-five dollars in the Come area for a new Come bet.

Chris, then, tossed the five dollar chip to the stick person and said, "Replace my Hard Six."

Meanwhile, Michael was paid thirty-five dollars for his Place bet on the Six, but lost his ten dollar Field bet, a net win of twenty-five dollars.

The next roll of the dice was a five and four, "Nine, center Field Nine," the stick person called out.

The dealer took the twenty-five dollars from the Come area and moved it inside of the box marked "Nine." Chris tossed the dealer one hundred dollars and said, "Odds for my Nine, please."

Chris put another twenty-five dollars in the Come area.

Michael was paid fourteen dollars for his ten dollar Place bet on the Nine and won ten dollars for his ten dollar Field bet; a net win of twenty-four dollars. He then told the dealer to turn his bets off. Chris was perplexed by Michael's betting. He thought "Again with turning his bets off."

The next roll of the dice was a pair of sixes. The stick person called out, "Box cars, Twelve, take the Come and pay the Field three times the bet.

Players who made Field bets were ecstatic because they

were paid triple. Chris didn't say a word. He lost his twenty-five dollar Come bet.

One player tossed a red five dollar red chip to the stick person and yelled out, "Horn high 'Yo'." Michael tossed out a five dollar chip and said, "Five dollar Horn high 'Yo' for me, as well."

A Horn bet is a one roll bet on the Two, Three, Eleven and Twelve. A Horn high "Yo" bet meant the extra dollar was bet on the Eleven (craps slang, "Yo"). So the player with the five dollar Horn high "Yo" bet was actually betting one dollar on the Two, Three and Twelve and two dollars on the Eleven. Michael also placed ten dollars in the Field.

Chris glared at Michael. He put a twenty-five dollar chip in the Come area. Michael didn't acknowledge Chris and did not care about Chris putting a green twenty-five dollar chip in the Come area. To Michael, the Come bet was the worst bet a player could make. To Chris, a Field bet was the worst bet a player could make. Each had their own opinions of how to play the game.

The shooter's next roll came up snake eyes, aces on the faces; a pair of ones. "Pay double in the Field, take the Come," the stick man yelled out.

Michael and the player who made the Horn high "Yo" bet were each paid twenty-six dollars for their wagers. Michael was also paid doubled for his ten dollar Field bet, another twenty dollars, a net win of forty-six dollars. Michael picked up his winnings. The Horn high "Yo" bets remained.

Michael looked at Chris and smiled. Chris was not amused having just lost another twenty-five dollars on his Come bet.

The shooter next rolled a six and one, the stick person

called out "Six and one this shooter's done, Seven out, line away. Again, the dealers' swept all of the chips on the table towards them and stacked them in the casino's bank.

Chris was pissed. The Seven came before any numbers were repeated. He lost all of his bets, a net total loss of five hundred and fifteen dollars on that shooter.

Michael was up approximately one hundred fifty dollars. He put all of his chips in front of him and said, "Color up." Chris watched as the dealer pushed Michael's stack of chips to the box person to be counted.

The box person counted the chips and called out, "Six hundred and fifty dollars." The dealer pushed the balance of chips to Michael. Michael picked up the chips and tossed a five dollar chip on the table and said, "For the dealers." He walked away from the table with a slight smile on his face, more of a smirk.

Chris colored up his chips, as well. He had a net loss of almost six hundred dollars for his play at the table. He then asked the dealer something quietly. The dealer shook his head and whispered back to Chris. Chris thanked the dealer and headed toward the Cashier's cage to catch up with Michael.

As Chris walked away from the cashier he was still baffled by what had just happened. "How could you lose almost six hundred dollars in such a short period of time!!" he thought. Chris looked up to see Michael walking away from the cashier. He approached Michael and asked, "Hey, how did you know those shooters were going to roll a Seven?"

Michael turned to Chris, "I didn't. I just felt like it was time to take my bets down." Michael extended his hand to shake Chris', "I'm Michael Caldwell."

Chris shook Michael's hand and said, "Chris Rouser, nice

to meet you." Chris continued the conversation as the two continued to walk away from the Cashier's cage, "What kind of messed up betting method are you playing?" he asked.

Michael replied devoid of any emotion, "Mine."

Chris was to say the least, intrigued. "Can I buy you a drink? I'd like to learn more about what you're doing?"

Michael smiled and said, "Why not?"

The lounge area of Mandalay Bay was relatively quiet for a Tuesday evening at four thirty. Michael and Chris each ordered a Michelob Lite draft beer. Chris didn't say much at first. Michael remained silent and enjoyed the ice cold beer. Finally Chris broke the silence, "What method are you betting? I've never seen a player turn off his bets as quickly as you do."

Michael eyed Chris and said, "I keep it simple. I make certain bets based on what I observe at the table. People think the dice are just random. But over the years I have observed certain patterns and correlations that for whatever reason improve my chances of winning. For instance, when the Twelve was rolled I bet the Horn numbers."

Michael looked at Chris and asked, "You do know what a Horn number is right?"

Chris said, "Of course I do."

Michael, not sure Chris was following what he was saying, asked Chris, "Okay, what are the Horn numbers?"

Chris answered, "Horn numbers are the Two, Three, Eleven and Twelve."

"Excellent," Michael said. He continued, "I've noticed over the years that Horn numbers seem to repeat or come in pairs. Sometimes I'm wrong and it will skip a number. I'm right about sixty-five percent of the time. That's why I bet the Horn high 'Yo' for five dollars. I won twenty-six dollars you lost your

Come bet."

The other thing I do, Michael said, "I usually only leave my bets for one or two rolls after a shooter establishes a point."

"Why is that?" Chris asked now more curious than ever. Michael explained, "Based on *mathematical* probability a Seven should appear once every six rolls. But we do not know if the Seven will appear on the first roll, second roll, third roll, or it could appear two or three times after the tenth roll. It is similar to flipping a coin, just because a head should appear fifty times out of one hundred flips doesn't mean it will happen. There may be times when a tail will appear sixty times and a head forty times during a hundred flips or vice versa. The probability is based on infinity."

"Based on *statistics*, however, the *average* shooter will usually have a *decision* within 3.37 rolls after establishing a point. What that means is that the shooter will either roll a Seven or make his point. In the event he rolls a Seven, I want to be on the right side of the shooter before he rolls a Seven out. It costs nothing for me to watch - - and it may add to my comp time for play. If I am right I do not lose money. If I am wrong it costs me nothing to watch. Also, with many of the betting tactics I utilize, it will take me four to six winning rolls to make up for one loss on a Seven out. The person who stays up for an extra three to six rolls may actually win more rolls, but make less money."

"Let me give you an example," Michael said. "Player A and Player B are going to make the exact same bets. Both are going to wait for a point to be established and then bet twenty-five dollars on the Five and thirty dollars on the Six and Eight each. Plus they will both make a fifteen dollar Field bet, a total Both Player A and Player B will lose their fifteen dollar Field bet, combined bet of one hundred dollars. For illustration purposes, the shooters first roll after establishing a point of Four is Five. but they will each win thirty-five dollars for their Place bet on the Five; a net win of twenty dollars. Both Players replace their fifteen dollar Field bet. The next roll is a Nine. Both Players win fifteen dollars in the Field. Player A tells the dealer to take his bets down. He has locked up a net win of thirty-five dollars."

"Player B thinks the attractive female shooter is a hot shooter and keeps his bets working. The next roll of the dice is a Six. Shooter B makes another twenty dollar net win and replaces his Field bet. The next roll is an Eight. Again Player B wins another twenty dollars. Player B is on a roll and thinks Player A is a wuss, and an idiot for missing a great roll. The next roll is an Eleven. Player B wins fifteen dollars for his Field bet. He is up a total of ninety dollars. The next roll is a Seven out. Player B just lost all of his profits plus ten dollars of his initial bet."

"Meanwhile, Player A still had his thirty-five dollar profit. So while Player B won more often, Player A made more money. Remember, they were both making the exact same bet. If you can wrap your mind around this concept, you can consistently win at craps. *If you can't, you're just another gambler.*"

Chris was sold. He had reached the end of his wits. It might just be time to let go of his old train of thought and embrace a new one. He asked if they could meet again the next day so that he could learn Michael's secret of how to make money playing craps. If Michael was willing to teach, he was willing to learn. "When the student is ready, the teacher will appear."

Michael had come to Vegas alone and agreed to meet with Chris the next day. After all, how often do you get to hang out with a former NFL superstar? Michael warned Chris that what he was about to learn took him many years of patience and discipline at the tables and that it could not be learned overnight or over a few days. What Michael had created were habits. We all have habits, some good some bad. Habits are subconscious actions, we do them automatically. These habits, of course, are formed over time. No one picks up a cigarette one day and becomes hooked on nicotine. But if they smoke on consecutive days, multiple times per day over time... a habit is formed. Good habits are formed the same way. Author Jeff Olson calls it, "The Slight Edge." Small simple daily disciplines done over time compound into huge results. This is the **INNER-GAME** of craps. Most people do not have the patience or the discipline to create the good habits of playing craps.

We live in an instant gratification society where we want what we want, and we want it RIGHT NOW! Hollywood and Madison Avenue would lead you to believe that you can have anything you want, right now or over the course of a ninety minute movie. That's fantasy!! If you want to live in a fantasy world, go to your favorite casino, play craps without patience, discipline, good habits and you will go home BROKE, end of story.

"When fantasy meets reality... REALITY WINS."
                                                    –Mark Jackson

Chapter TWO

Fundamentally Sound

In the background of the Wynn Casino was a commotion of loud, intricate, and convoluted noise. The one-arm bandits made the sound of silver dollar coins dropping into the metallic tray with clings and clatter. Beautiful cocktail waitresses wearing skimpy outfits called out, "Cocktails" to the patrons as they walked around the casino floor. The roulette wheel spun in silent motion as the ball whirled around the side until finally landing on a number. Cards shuffled at the blackjack tables made a fluttering sound.

Back at the craps table, a middle aged lady tossed the dice. As they spun around and bounced back off the opposite wall, the stickperson called out, "Six, mark the point, the point is Six – mark it."

Michael was at the table just watching the action when Chris approached him. "Thanks for agreeing to meet with me, Michael," Chris said. The two shook hands as Michael suggested they talk in a quiet place. They made their way to the sports deli.

"How can I help you?" Michael asked.

"I didn't sleep much last night thinking about how I saw you play at that table and what you told me. It seems like I learned the game of craps all wrong. I learned the way the house teaches. Of course, the house isn't going to teach people how to beat them," Chris replied.

Michael chuckled and in a sarcastic tone said, "Ya think?" After a brief discussion Michael needed to learn if Chris was teachable and what knowledge he had of the game of craps. Surprisingly, Chris knew a lot more than the average person who plays the game.

"So what seems to be the problem?" Michael asked. Chris started telling Michael how he couldn't stop playing once he was up. "Often times I'd win within the first ten to fifteen minutes of playing but I found it difficult, if not impossible, to walk away from the table. I figured if I could win that easily and that quickly, I could continue." Michael kept listening. "I'm not sure if it's the competitive nature in me that is always looking to 'Break the House' and leave with five to ten times my buy in. That's my perception of winning." Chris was extremely competitive. He didn't like to quit.

Michael quickly realized that Chris did not set goals when playing craps and did not know when to walk away from the craps table. He lacked that discipline.

Michael began the conversation by explaining to Chris that he was there to make money, not to play craps. Craps was the vehicle he used to make his money. To Michael, playing craps was a business. To Chris it was a challenge.

Michael began, "First and foremost, treat craps as a business. In any business or profession, you would normally research and learn before investing your money. Why wouldn't you do the same before playing craps to make money? Gaming establishments will gladly teach you how to play any casino game. In fact, they hold classes in the casino to teach people how to make bets at the craps table. What they do not teach you is the mathematics of the game; reasons to make a bet or not to bet; when to take your bets down or 'turn them off' or techniques and strategies to win - - *the casinos only teach how to make a bet.* Do you believe that casino personnel will actually teach you how to win their money? Of course not!"

"Consider this: If the casino personnel actually knew how to win playing craps do you think they would be working for the casino? They would, undoubtedly, be playing craps professionally themselves."

"Speaking of professional craps players, yes, they do exist. Most of them will not advertise or tell you that is how they make their living, but they do exist."

"Before we get into how I play craps, how I bet and what types of bets to make, *it is important to learn to walk away from the tables when you're winning, whether it is craps, blackjack, roulette or any other type of gambling*. It is imperative that you have *mental, emotional, and psychological discipline*. It is vital that you understand and realize that winning is a process, you must set a specific, realistic and attainable goal of how much you want to win before you even walk up to a craps table. *Do not set a goal to win as much as possible*. This is not specific nor is it realistic. Simply stated, you must have a pre-determined, specific, 'realistic' and attainable goal of how much money you want to win each session or day before you start betting."

"Once you have reached your goal, you will know when to stop betting. There will be no guess work. Without a pre-determined objective, there is no plan. Without a plan, you will eventually give back the profits you earned and maybe even more to the casino. Making money is a serious business. So is losing money. You must have a plan and stick with the plan."

"It may take only a few minutes to reach your goal. It may take you a little longer. The most important thing to understand is that the longer you are at the table, the more likely you are to lose. Therefore, if you have not reached your goal within a pre-determined time, stop. It is better to have reached eighty percent or ninety percent of your objective than to lose money. Most of our sessions are limited to one (1) hour, usually less. Any longer and you start to get tired and fatigued."

"If you are tired, fatigued or hungry you cannot properly concentrate. Take time to rest. The casinos are not going anywhere. They are open twenty-four hours a day, seven days a week. So relax. Go shopping, lay out by the pool, see a show, have lunch or dinner depending on the time of day. There is a lot to do other than playing craps without a break."

"Having the right attitude is equally important. Most people who go to a casino have the attitude of taking a certain amount of money with them and when they lose they will stop, unless, of course, they withdraw more money from the ATM. This is a defeatist attitude and not conducive to winning. It is negative and is also a poor way to manage your money."

"Other people set a goal to make as much as possible. This is too vague and speculative. The human mind responds to specifics, it will help you to attain your goal when it knows exactly what the goal is. It will support you when it's clear. It is useless when confused. Remember, clarity is power. Most of the time people will stay too long at the table because how much is 'as much as possible?' How do you exactly define 'as much as possible?' Most people will stay too long at the craps table and lose everything they made and then some."

Michael explained that he took a different approach. He set a *specific, measurable, attainable* and *realistic* goal within a specific *time* parameter of how much he wanted to win and once he made that goal he stopped. He knew exactly when to walk away from the table. "Do you see the difference between these three attitudes?" he asked Chris. Chris started to learn basic concepts of winning, not just at craps, but any other game of chance.

> *"Goals need to be specific and measurable and have a time limit."* - - **Dave Ramsey**

So what is a realistic and attainable goal you may be wondering? In Michael's opinion, fifteen to twenty percent of the buy-in was realistic. For simplicity, let's say Chris bought in for one thousand dollars. His goal was to win between one hundred fifty and two hundred dollars. One hundred fifty dollars is fifteen percent of one thousand hundred. If Chris played two or three sessions per day, he'd earn three hundred dollars to six hundred dollars per day.

While winning between three hundred and six hundred dollars per day may not seem like a lot of money to some people, in reality, it is a lot of money for many other people. Since each person's financial situation is different, you can adjust this illustration to your own situation accordingly buying in for more or less.

In today's economy, many people are earning twelve to fifteen dollars per hour, working eight hours per day; usually for a business they do not like or a boss they hate. That means they are making between ninety-six and one hundred twenty dollars per eight hour day.

Winning three to six hundred dollars per day and playing over a three day weekend is equivalent to three to four weeks of slaving in a job! You've earned one thousand three hundred fifty dollars on the low side, eighteen hundred dollars on the high side. Most people would be thrilled to earn eight to twelve percent **annually** on their investments, let alone to earn that percentage daily. Does that sound impressive? By the way, if you have not done the calculation, an average of four hundred dollars per day working five days a week, fifty weeks a year (take two weeks off for vacation) is the equivalent of one hundred thousand dollars per year. Are you earning three or four hundred dollars per day? *Playing craps to earn a living is not glamorous. It is not the same as playing in the NFL. Just like playing in the NFL, it is hard work.* Like in the NFL, you must put in the time and effort to be successful. It is incredibly fun when you WIN!! Not so much fun when you lose.

John Patrick, in his book *John Patrick's Advanced Craps*, writes: "Seventy percent of craps players get ahead at one point in their casino visits. Of that seventy percent, ninety percent give back their winnings . . . and then some." John Patrick's message is to know when to walk away from the craps table.

Michael explained to Chris that his focus was to make playing craps profitable and to walk away with earnings. He said, "A person cannot play craps *'to simply have fun'* and expect to win. A person either plays to win or to have fun. The casinos catered to those who want to have fun. They, however, prefer to call it *'entertainment.'* While winning is fun, you cannot do both. People who make their goal in the first ten or fifteen minutes of play generally become bored or anxious. They want to play longer because they're having fun. If they are at the casino to play craps, what else are they going to do? Watch? Unlikely! Unless a person has the discipline to walk away with a profit, they most likely will be one of the players who give back their winnings to the casino as stated by John Patrick."

Michael continued to explain to Chris about making money playing craps. "Chris, let's go to the craps table and play for a short time. I will put up one thousand dollars if you will do the same. Chris agreed, and asked Michael, "Why is twenty percent a good goal to make per session? Why not thirty percent or fifty percent?" Michael's only answer was that twenty percent worked for him. The point is not so much about the percentage (as long as it is realistic); the point is that once you make your goal you *STOP!*

To prove his point, Chris and Michael went to the craps table with the goal to make twenty percent on a two thousand dollar buy-in (about four hundred dollars). Michael and Chris combined their funds and bought-in during the middle of a shooter's roll. After a few rolls the shooter rolled a craps number (Two, Three and Twelve are craps numbers). Michael made a hundred dollar Field bet, the next roll was a Twelve. They were paid three hundred dollars. They removed their winnings and took the Field bet down. A few rolls later another craps number was rolled. Michael (on behalf of himself and Chris) made another one hundred dollar Field bet. The next roll was a Four. They made another hundred dollars. Michael colored up their chips with a four hundred dollar profit - - they made their goal!

Chris asked Michael, "Why are you coloring-up?" Michael replied, "Because we made our goal. We are done."

Michael gave Chris one thousand two hundred dollars (one thousand dollar buy-in plus two hundred dollar profit). Chris, not satisfied with two hundred dollars, wanted to make more. "Michael, two hundred dollars is nothing. Why can't we play some more? We just got here."

"Because Chris, it is not the amount it is the goal. That is the premise of our entire lesson. Twenty percent is twenty percent. If you cannot make money playing with a small amount of money, you will not be able to make money playing with a large amount of money. It is all relative."

Chris did not listen to Michael. He wanted to make some

more money. He made a Pass Line bet for one hundred dollars. The next roll was a Seven. Chris promptly won one hundred dollars. He smiled at Michael. The shooter's next roll was a Six. Chris quickly placed two hundred fifty dollars behind the line for odds and tossed a twenty-five dollar chip to the stick person for a Hard Six. Chris made two more Come bets with odds on the next few rolls. The next roll after these, the shooter rolled a Seven out. Chris lost his Pass line bet, his odds and his Hard Six bet, and all of his other Come bets plus odds; a total of nine hundred seventy-five dollars. Michael tugged at Chris' arm and said "Let's go. We need to talk." Michael had a two hundred dollar profit; Chris had lost almost eight hundred dollars.

So what is the point behind this story? *It is simple - to leave the table once you made your goal no matter how quickly or how you made it.* There are many, many, many ways to win at the craps table. It does not matter how you win; it only matters how much you walk away with after you win.

There is an adage about scuba divers that says "There are old divers and there are bold divers, but there are no old bold divers." In craps, there are players who play for fun and there are players who play to win, but there are no players who play for fun who consistently win. I can assure you that while it is fun to win, it is not fun to lose.

Michael believed that playing craps to earn money was work and was not for fun. It was not glamorous. It was not exciting. It was work!

"Chris, please don't be insulted, but I want to start from the beginning just so you and I are the same page," Michael said. Chris nodded in agreement. He was there to listen and learn.

"First, you need to apply the discipline you used in the NFL to playing craps. Second, you will need to study the game of craps and put in as much effort to learning as you did studying your play book. If you can do this, I can help you. If not, you are wasting your time and mine."

Michael and Chris sat in the Wynn's sports lounge. Michael bought a round of beers. "Look, Chris, what I do to make money is the most difficult thing you can imagine. Today was a perfect example. What was the reason for you losing and my winning? I stopped after reaching our goal of twenty percent. Why did you lose? You lost, because you were greedy and wanted to win more. It is that simple. Chris, I do not play craps to make a 'killing' or a big 'score.' There are days when people make a hell of lot more money at craps than I do. There are days when I make more than they do. The most important lesson I can teach you is that craps is how I make money. As a good friend of mine said, 'No person ever went broke taking a profit.' Like I mentioned earlier, twenty percent return on my buy-in works for me. If twenty percent return on your money in one day does not work for you, you may want to think of earning money some other way than craps."

Chapter THREE

Probability Matters

Michael continued Chris' lesson, "All casino games are based on probability models. Probability models are used to determine the odds on the various betting scenarios. Probability models are based on infinity and they project various outcomes for certain games. For example, if you toss a coin one hundred times, the probability model provides that there will be fifty heads for every fifty tails. Each game has its own probability model."

"Craps is played with two dice. Each die has six sides numbered one through six. Thus, each cube has six equal independent possible outcomes when thrown. Two dice thrown together have a total number of thirty-six (36) possible outcomes: the number Seven (7) has the highest probability of occurring by random throw of the two dice, being the sum of six possible combinations; next in frequency are the Six (6) and Eight (8), having five possible combinations each; the Five (5) and Nine (9) have four possible combinations of the dice; Four (4) and Ten (10) result from three possible combinations of the dice; Three (3) and Eleven (11) result from two possible combinations of the dice; and the Two (2) and Twelve (12) have only one combination each." [Shown at the end of this chapter is an illustration of the probability model of these combinations.]

"Because of disproportionate occurrences, random events occur sporadically. Simply stated, **streaks are disproportionate occurrences. Streaks happen when the probability models do not work in the short run.** I'll explain. If you toss a coin there are two possible outcomes: heads or tails. The probability of a heads appearing is one in two, or fifty percent. The same is true for tails. Over an infinite number of trials, the results should be fifty percent of the time heads will appear and fifty percent of the time tails will appear."

"However, if you toss a coin one hundred times, there may be twenty heads and eighty tails. There may be streaks when the tails occurs significantly more than the heads. The next one hundred coin tosses may result in forty-five heads and fifty-five tails. Yet, the next one hundred tosses may result in eighty heads and only twenty tails. Overall, out of three hundred tosses, the heads and tails did appear an approximately equal number of times. Very, very, very, very, rarely, will one hundred coin tosses result in exactly fifty heads and fifty tails. ***Probability is based on theory and not reality.***"

"If you spin a roulette wheel, there are thirty-eight equal possible outcomes: numbers one through thirty-six, zero and double zero; eighteen 'Red' numbers, eighteen 'Black' numbers, and two 'Green' numbers: '0' and '00." Since there are thirty-eight numbers on the roulette wheel, each number has the same probability of being spun (1 in 38 or 2.63%; the probability of a 'Red' number being spun is 18 in 38 or 47.37% and the probability of a 'Black' number being spun is the same, 18 in 38 or 47.37%. Over an infinite number of spins the results should be that each number will be spun at least once every thirty-eight spins of the wheel. In real life this does not occur. That is why they call it gambling."

"Also, if the odds are 1 in 38 of any particular number and the house pays you 36 for 1 there is a 5.26% edge for the house. This edge is how they build multi-million dollar casinos! Five percent (5%) of 10 billion dollars is fifty million dollars ($50,000,000). You've heard the saying, "Vegas was not built on winners." Ask any cabbie and they'll tell you Vegas was built on fear and greed."

"If the probability models worked in the short run as in the long run, the casinos would have been out of business a long time ago. There would be no challenge because we would already know the outcome based on the probability models working in the short run as they do over the long run, i.e., an infinite period of time. Casinos rely on the disproportionate occurrences (streaks) during shorter periods of time when gamblers play (a shorter period of time in my opinion is anything less than twenty-four hours straight). The casinos operate twenty-four hours per day, seven days per week, fifty two weeks per year, year after year after year. A person cannot properly function at the tables for more than a few hours."

"The Gambler's Fallacy, also referred to as the *doctrine of the maturity of chances*, and is the belief that a departure from what occurs on average or in the long term will be corrected in the short term. The fallacy is committed when someone assumes that some result must occur or is 'due' to happen simply because of what has happened departed from what would be expected on average or over the long term. When an individual erroneously believes that a certain random event is more or less likely to happen because of what occurred on a prior event or a series of events that is a 'Gambler's Fallacy.' How many times have you seen black appear on a roulette wheel for ten, eleven, twelve or more consecutives spins and over heard some person say 'Red has got to hit!' This line of thinking is incorrect because past events do not change the probability that certain events will occur in the future."

"There are people who, after several flips of a coin in which heads appears, will always bet tails believing that 'It is due.' Similarly, there are craps players who bet either the Don't Pass or Don't Come if a shooter has made several numbers or passes thinking, 'He can't make another one.' But they do and the player loses."

By the time Michael had finished his probability lecture Chris's head was spinning. An hour had passed. Michael suggested that they take a break and meet back in a few hours so Chris could absorb what Michael was teaching him.

PROBABILITY MODEL FOR CRAPS

There are 36 possible combinations for two dice!

Number	Combinations	Ways to Roll	Probability	
2	One	1:1	2.78%	(1/36)
3	Two	2:1, 1:2	5.56%	(2/36)
4	Three	3:1, 1:3, 2:2	8.33%	(3/36)
5	Four	4:1, 1:4, 3:2, 2:3	11.11%	(4/36)
6	Five	5:1, 1:5, 4:2, 2:4, 3:3	13.89%	(5/36)
7	Six	6:1, 1:6, 5:2, 2:5, 3:4, 4:3	16.67%	(6/36)
8	Five	2:6, 3:5, 4:4, 5:3, 6:2	13.89%	(5/36)
9	Four	3:6, 4:5, 5:4, 6:3	11.11%	(4/36)
10	Three	4:6, 5:5, 6:4	8.33%	(3/36)
11	Two	5:6, 6:5	5.56%	(2/36)
12	One	6:6	2.78%	(1/36)

Chapter FOUR

The Lesson

"Are you ready to learn some more?" Michael asked Chris. Chris was more than ready. The probability lesson had sunk in. He was beginning to have a new appreciation of what he needed to do to win at playing craps. He was ready to devote more time and attention to master the game of craps. Michael told Chris he was going to start with a very simple and basic betting method, the "Iron Cross." Chris demonstrated that he was sincere in what Michael was teaching him and took out a note pad and pen to take notes. Michael smiled as he saw Chris now becoming a student of the game.

The "Iron Cross," Michael began, "Is making a bet on the Five, Six and Eight and one-half of the payout on the Field. (The "Iron Cross" was developed by **Jerry Patterson** - -However, Michael's ideas of how to utilize this particular bet are different than those of Mr. Patterson).

"There are various betting levels you can utilize with this strategy depending on the size of your bankroll and how knowledgeable and confident you are with betting. *This strategy is based on making only two bets after the shooter establishes a point.* The bets are placed only after the shooter establishes a point. For example, if the shooter's first Come out roll is a Two you do not make a bet. If the next roll is a Seven, you still do not make a bet. You wait until the shooter establishes a point. What the shooter rolls on the Come-out roll will determine if you make any bets at all on the particular shooter. For instance, *if a shooter rolls two or three Sevens (7's) on the Come-out roll, generally you should not make a bet on this shooter.*" Michael mentioned that his experience has been that the shooter will normally establish a point and then Seven out. He has been wrong and sometimes the shooter has long rolls. But that has not happened too often. Michael then explained that bets are made as follows:

1. Before placing any bets, look for a table that is at least half-full of players betting on numbers. Sometimes a table will look crowded but it may be that there are a lot of people just watching and not making bets. A table that is at least half-full with people actually making bets is an indication that a number other than a Seven is being rolled. In general, if a table is cold or choppy (a table where shooters are rolling a Seven out early during their roll) players leave to go to other tables.

2. This betting strategy does not involve the Come-out roll. Do **not** place any bets on the Pass Line or Don't Pass Line. The "Come-out" roll is the first roll of the dice by a shooter before any point is established. You can always tell when it is a "Come-out" roll because the puck used to mark the point is on the Don't Come area of the layout and the side marked "OFF" is upright. After the shooter establishes a point, whether it be the Four (4), Five (5), Six (6), Eight (8), Nine (9) or Ten (10), the dealer will move the puck to that number and flip it over from the "OFF" position to the "ON" position indicating the point.

3. **After** the shooter establishes a point, make a Place bet on the Five, Six, Eight and Field. At most casinos in downtown Vegas, the minimum bet is five dollars. For illustration purposes we will consider the lowest level of betting for this method to be at a five dollars table. Therefore, you would make a Place bet on the Five for ten

dollars, a Place bet on the Six and Eight each for twelve and a Field bet for seven dollars. By making bets on the Five, Six, Eight and Field you are covering every paying or good number. Of course, once a point is established all Place bets and Field bets lose with the roll of a Seven. A bet on the Field will cover the numbers Two, Three, Four, Nine, Ten, Eleven, and Twelve. *See Figure 1.*

FIGURE 1 ("Iron Cross bet")

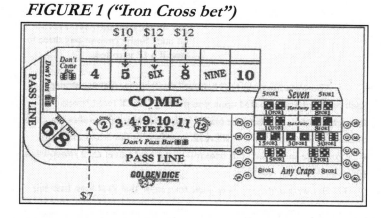

4.   For illustration purposes, let's assume the shooter establishes a point of Four. You bet ten dollars on the Five, twelve dollars on the Six and Eight each and seven dollars on the Field. If the next roll of the shooter is an Eight, you lose your Field bet of seven dollars but win fourteen dollars on the Eight, a net win of seven dollars. If the shooter's roll was a Nine instead of an Eight, you would win your Field bet of seven dollars. Your bets on the Five, Six and Eight are not affected. If perhaps the shooter rolled a Two or Twelve you would win either double or triple your Field bet of seven dollars depending on the layout of the table. Some casinos pay double for a two in the Field, while others pay triple. Other casinos

pay double for a two and triple for a Twelve. It varies so pay attention to the layout.

5. If a Five, Six or Eight are rolled on the first roll immediately after the shooter establishes a point, you need to replace your Field bet. You do the same thing for one more roll and then take all of your bets down and wait for the next shooter. Waiting for the shooter to Seven-out requires a lot of discipline and can be trying at times. The hardest part for Chris was being at a table where Michael removed his bets only to watch the shooter keep rolling number after number after number.

Michael continued, "You must always make a Place bet on the five in multiples of Five dollars and make Place bets on the Six and Eight in multiples of six dollars. The reason is that a Place bet on the Five is always paid off at a ratio of seven to five. Bet five dollars, get paid seven dollars. Likewise, you must always make a Place bet on the Six or Eight in multiples of six dollars because the Place bets on the Six and Eight are paid off at a ratio of seven to six. Bet six dollars, get paid seven dollars. So if you bet ten dollars on the Five and twelve dollars on the Six and Eight each, each number will pay fourteen dollars. The Field bet should be approximately one-half of the pay-off of the Five, Six and Eight. Thus, one-half of fourteen dollars is seven dollars, so you would bet seven dollars on the Field."

"If the shooter makes two numbers, take all bets down and wait until the next shooter. Your bets will remain on the table unless you ask the dealer to take them down. This is extremely important to remember especially if you are making larger bets. If you do not ask the dealer to take down your bets and the shooter rolls a Seven, you will lose the total of your combined bets. So, you must remember to ask the dealer to take down your bets after your second win."

"If the shooter makes his point, then the same shooter *may* become a new shooter, but not always. If a shooter makes his point, I do not bet again on the same shooter. In other words, I *do not* consider him/her to be a '*new shooter,*' Many times a shooter will make his point within the first few rolls (less than ten rolls) of the dice and then *after establishing a new point*, immediately Seven-out. Maintaining a strict discipline is extremely important."

"The probability of winning using the Five, Six, Eight and Field is as follows: There are thirty-six possible outcomes from any particular roll of the dice. There are thirty (30) ways to make the Five, Six, Eight and Field and six ways to make the Seven. Thus on any given roll of the dice there are 30/36 ways to win (a probability of 83.3%) and 6/36 possible combinations of the dice to make a Seven, in which you lose (a probability of 16.7%). You are betting a larger amount of money to win a smaller amount, but with a higher probability of winning."

Chris interjected, "That's it? What about missing a hot shooter and making a killing?"

Michael flashed a wicked smile at Chris, "So what if I miss a hot shooter. By the time you're waiting to make your killing I'm up a hundred or two and out of the casino. The difference between me and most other craps players is I'm here to make money, not to play craps. Craps is just the vehicle I use to make money. You on the other hand get an adrenalin rush from the action. That's not playing to make money, that's being there for the excitement. There is a big difference."

The lesson continued with Michael explaining that his good friend and craps buddy, **"B.K." taught him a different variation of the Iron Cross bet.** *B.K. is not only a craps guru* *he is the greatest craps player.* It was a "Modified Iron Cross."

"The 'Modified Iron Cross' is a bet wherein you bet ten dollars on the Four, twenty-five dollars on the Five, thirty dollars on the Six and Eight each, ten dollars on the Nine and Ten, plus ten dollars in the Field. The total combined bet is one hundred twenty-five dollars. The idea is to make an average of twenty-five dollars on each roll of the dice. The exception being that if an Eleven or Three is rolled you only make ten dollars on the Field bet."

"In essence here is how it works, if a Four is rolled, the player will win eighteen dollars on the ten dollar Place bet on the Four, plus ten dollars for the Field bet, a total of twenty-eight dollars. The same applies to the Ten. If a Five, Six or Eight is rolled the player will win thirty-five dollars for those Place bets, but lose his ten dollar Field bet, a net win of twenty-five dollars. If a Two or Twelve is rolled, the shooter will win either twenty or thirty dollars for the Field bet depending on the layout at each casino. If a Three or Eleven is rolled, the shooter will win ten dollars for the Field bet."

Chris's interest was piqued by Michael's calmness and rational for making money playing craps. "How much do you make with your betting method?" Chris asked.

Michael thought for a moment before answering Chris's question. Then he asked, "Are you with the IRS?"

Chris laughed out loud and said, "Hell no. Do I look like I work for the IRS?"

Michael said, "No, not really." He took another swig of beer.

Chris pressed the issue. He asked Michael again, "Seriously, how much do you make playing craps?"

Michael's answer was much along the lines of any guru,

"It depends on how much I'm willing to risk. I don't believe that craps is well suited for a person who is desperate or really needs to make lots of money fast. And so it is with life, get rich quick schemes are usually just that . . . schemes. My methods of playing craps yield consistent results over time much like a guy who is adept at playing the stock market. He gets in and out of trades, locking in small profits and over time, his earning compound into massive wealth." Michael now asked Chris a simple question, "How do you eat an elephant?" Perplexed by the question, Chris' response was "WHAT?? How many beers have you had??" "How do you eat an elephant?" Michael persisted. Before Chris could give a nonsense answer Michael said, "One –bite –at –a – time!"

Michael was amused with Chris and his fascination with his betting philosophy and said, "I'm not convinced you have the discipline and self control to do what I do. I tell people that only one or two percent of all of the people who play craps can do what I do. It's simple, but not easy to execute. And of course everyone thinks they are in that one or two percent."

Chris listened to what Michael was saying. He knew deep down inside that Caldwell was spot on about the discipline of the game. Chris had himself overcome tremendous odds to play in the NFL for nine years. It would take an entirely different skill set to accomplish what Michael had accomplished. Chris loved the rush of the action. He loved the competition. Winning was always an added bonus. Subconsciously he could care less if he lost because he loved the action of the game. That's the INNER-GAME flaw that spells disaster for most people that play the game of craps. If walking away with a profit is not the sole purpose of each gaming session, you lose. One percent of doubt and you're out!! "A little faith can go a long way to accomplishing whatever endeavors you desire. A little doubt will destroy your dreams or worse, it will kill you."

Still, Chris said to Michael, "Teach me as much as you can as fast as you can. Let me worry about the rest."

Michael asked Chris, "Just how much do you want to make?"

Chris smirked and casually replied, "Ten thousand in four weeks."

Michael put his beer down and looked at Chris in disbelief, "Are you out of your freakin mind?"

Chris smiled and said matter of fact, "No, I'm dead serious."

Michael asked him, "What kind of bankroll you got?" Chris answered, "How much do I need?"

Michael thought for a moment, pulled out a pen from his jacket pocket and made some quick calculations on his drink napkin. Ten thousand divided by twenty days equaled five hundred a day. Five hundred a day divided by three sessions a day equaled a little more than one hundred sixty-five dollars each session played assuming everything went perfect.

Michael shot back at Chris, "You're going to need a ten thousand dollar bankroll." Michael hoped the number would scare off Chris. Much to Michael's chagrin Chris responded, "No problem. Meet me back here tonight at eleven sharp so we can get started."

Michael asked Chris a fair question, "If you already have a ten thousand dollar bankroll, why do you need to make ten thousand dollars in the next month? Seems to me you already have it?"

Chris was reluctant to tell Michael the true purpose of why he really needed the money. It was nothing sinister or devious.

Chris was a private person and wanted to keep it that way, especially since he hardly knew Michael inasmuch as they just met. He thought about it and answered Michael, "I need twenty thousand dollars in total. I have the ten and need to double it. Can you help me do that? Yes or no?"

Michael smiled and said, "Maybe. It is mostly up to you."

Michael left Chris. He walked away wondering what nightmare he was about to enter. Chris, on the other hand, heard a voice in his head saying, "Be true unto yourself and in the end you will awake to rise up and be free and live happily. In this way you'll come to understand that the evil and the good had all been misunderstood." Chris had no clue what any of this meant.

Michael had suggested that they back off the subject of 'How can I win' for a while. "I have tickets to the Cirque Show — Le Reve, would you like to join me??" Michael offered. "Sure" Chris replied with little enthusiasm. He wanted to get back on the tables and felt watching a show was a waste of time. Michael continued, "Meet me here at six-thirty and we'll grab a bite to eat then hit the show together. It'll be a great time to relax your mind and let some of the information I've been sharing sink in."

Chapter FIVE

The Ah-ha Moment

Chris arrived at six o'clock in the evening excited to glean more from Michael. For once, he felt he had a chance at success and could get off the craps rollercoaster that he'd been on. Win, lose. Win, lose even more. Lose, lose…

Chris called Michael. "I'm here." "Hey Chris I'm running a little behind schedule. Why don't you come up to the room?" Michael replied. "I'll meet you at the elevators you'll need a key to get past the guards." Once they got back to the room Chris couldn't believe his eyes. He'd been in many fine hotels all over the world but this two bedroom suite took the cake. With a spectacular view of the strip and all the creature comforts!! "Grab a drink at the bar if you'd like, I'll just be a minute." Michael directed Chris. "I'm a whiskey man, Gentlemen's Jack – Bullet –Wolsford but I believe there are Grey Goose and Tanqueray, as well. The mixers are in the fridge."

Chris poured himself a drink and began munching on some of the fresh fruit, cheese crackers and nuts there on the counter. "Nice suite! Do you mind if I take a look around." Chris asked. "Suit yourself!" Michael yelled from the other room. Chris explored the second room; plasma TV screens everywhere, even in the bathroom across from the Jacuzzi tub and multi-head shower. There were several remote tablets that controlled everything from lighting, music, the TV and curtains?? Now THIS is how you do Vegas, he thought. Then he realized that on previous trips he may have spent four to five hours max in his room: too busy grinding it out on the tables. Just as he sat down on the plush sofa back in the main area, Michael popped out.

"Let's do this!!" He yelled with a zest for life. "Where's my drink? And here I thought we were becoming friends??" Michael said with a big grin on his face. He poured a cocktail and off they went.

As they headed down in the elevator, Michael asked, "Chinese, Italian or Steak House? What is your favorite food?" "I think I can do sushi" Chris replied.

"Excellent choice! You'll love ---- You know, Steve Wynn has an incredible art collection? The crystal wall decoration is said to cost millions to hang and it costs hundreds of thousands just to clean it. Guess what, that's nothing compared to the food, it's to die for," Michael said with a big laugh.

Once seated, Michael asked, "So, what would you like to eat?" Chris responded, "I'm not sure, I haven't seen the menu."

"Damn the menu, what would you like to eat? The chefs here are some of the best in the world. Do you believe that they can prepare 'whatever' it is that you'd like to eat?" Michael asked with a big smile on his face.

At that moment, the light came on for Chris. Despite all the money he had made in the NFL. Despite all the places he had traveled to, all the things he had experienced, he had never had this mindset –The Guru's mindset of "The world is your oyster –why limit yourself."

"How about you tell our waiter the types of fish you like without the menu, Sashimi, Tapenyaki, whatever, and let the chef surprise us!" Michael was like a little child. The waiter and chef were pleased to oblige. The food came out in stages of mouthwatering, exotic treats one after another. They had to stop after a while for fear of missing the show. Michael quickly signed the check to his room and off they hustled to catch it.

When they arrived they were escorted to premium seating.

Each seat was plush and equipped with a TV screen at the foot where you could enjoy footage of the show below the stage level. Drinks were served, and the show began. ....

After a thunderous applause Chris sat exhausted, his senses heightened by one death defying acrobatic maneuver after another. The show was almost too much for a person to experience. .... "So, how did you like the show?" Michael asked. "I have never experienced anything like that in my life," Chris responded still mesmerized. "What an experience."

Chapter SIX

Sun Tzu and Art of War

It was about eleven o'clock p.m. as they approached the craps tables. Michael told Chris that he had to watch before he could play. Learn by watching before using real money. Michael told Chris that whatever Michael told him meant nothing. But if Chris personally observed something and understood the meaning behind it then it meant everything. This was one of Michaels's conditions for him to teach Chris. Chris was agreeable. No money would be wagered that night. There was plenty of time to make the money Chris wanted to earn.

"Chris, have you read Sun Tzu's Art of War?" Michael asked. Chris responded that he did not know Sun Tzu or the "Art of War."

Michael believed with all of his heart that it was imperative for Chris to learn about Sun Tzu and understand the principles taught by him in the "Art of War." Michael made it another condition for Chris to learn Sun Tzu and the "Art of War" as it applied to playing craps if he was to continue to teach him how to master the game.

Sun Tzu advocated that there must be enough resources to sustain the operations of war. Similarly, funds must be available before the attack is launched. Translated to playing craps, *you should play with money you can afford to risk to lose and to make certain you have enough of a bankroll and/or buy-in to be able to reach a specific, realistic and attainable goal.*

Michael continued, "What is the major reason for every business failure?" The answer is usually, 'We ran out of money before we perfected the art of making money.' Ninety percent of all business failures are due to lack of capital or being under-capitalized. What is the major reason most players lose? They run out of money before a 'hot' shooter appears."

In every battle, the one with the most resources has the odds in his favor. Damon Runyon said, "The battle may not go to the strong, or the race to the swift, but that's the way to bet." The casinos have the upper-hand against the average craps player because they have superior resources (capital/money). The problem of adequate resources (capital/money) is that most craps players do not have enough money to withstand adverse outcomes based on the roll of the dice. To make matters worse, the average craps player will immediately increase his bets when he is losing in an attempt to recoup losses when he should be betting smaller or waiting for a more opportune time to make a large bet. This is sometimes referred to as "chasing."

Another superior resource the casino has over the average craps player is that the casino can operate the craps table twenty-four hours per day, seven days per week, every week of the year. The game of craps, as well as other casino games, is based on infinity. The average craps player cannot play for more than a few hours at a time and think clearly or function properly. After a few hours the average craps player will become fatigued. Know your own limits. After only one hour a break may be needed. When a person is fatigued they tend to make costly mistakes.

To achieve success, you must have superiority. Superiority, however, is relative. **To accomplish superiority over the casino it is only necessary to understand that you do not need to make a wager on every shooter and every roll of the dice. You have the right to be selective as to how much and when to bet.** Thus, the age old adage - - "how do you eat an elephant? The answer is one bite at a time." So it is with playing craps. How do you win at craps? The answer is one chip at a time. The casino, for the most part, must accept a player's bet. The casino does have the right to refuse a player's action, but this is very rare and usually when the player is either cheating or doing something suspicious.

A plan is useless unless it is properly executed. How the plan is executed is equally important. One of the principles advocated by Sun Tzu in executing a plan is swiftness. This is, of course, contrary to Sun Tzu's views on planning, where thoroughness and attention to detail would necessitate that the process take longer. The dice move quickly at the craps table. You must be prepared to make your bets and instruct the dealer accordingly. If you give the wrong instructions to the dealer, the best betting strategy will, more often than not, lose. You cannot be indecisive! You cannot be fumbling with your chips trying to get a bet made. If you are not quick with your execution of the bets you want to make the dice will have already been passed to the shooter and be in the air.

Unfortunately, unlike some concepts used in poker, blackjack or roulette, it is not easy to teach someone the application of timing what bets to make. This is because it is as much an art as it is a science. A lot depends on the judgment and experience of the player. While timing cannot be taught like a science, the art of applying it can be improved when one has more experience, and a better feel for table conditions and what is occurring at the table.

Michael repeated his earlier example for emphasis. "There are two players at the table standing next to each other *making the exact same bets*. Both players are making bets on the Five, Six, Eight and Field. With this combination (known as an 'Iron Cross' bet) it will take six wins to make up for one losing roll.

For illustration purposes, the total combined bet is one hundred dollars and the player will win an average of fifteen dollars for each winning roll of the dice. Player "A" decides to take his bets down after two rolls of the dice - - a net win of thirty dollars. Player "B," meanwhile, decides to let his bets remain working. Player "B" feels this is a "hot" shooter. The shooter rolls the dice again and Player "B" wins again. The next roll of the dice is another winning roll for Player "B." The shooter rolls the dice again, and Player "B" wins again. At this point Player "A" just watches. Player "B" thinks he is on a streak and will win a lot more than Player "A" on this shooter. Player "B" (at this time is up eighty-five dollars) goes so far as to tell Player "A" "You need to keep your bets working." On the very next roll of the dice, the dealer shouts "Seven out, line away." Player "B" loses all of his bets - - a total of one hundred dollars. *Upon further analysis, Player "A," actually won more money, despite Player "B" winning more bets*. Player "A" won thirty dollars and Player "B" lost fifteen dollars. **This is an important lesson. You can win more battles and still lose the war. It is not how often you win, but how much you keep.** **SOMETIMES BY MAKING FEWER BETS YOU CAN ACTUALLY WIN MORE."**

What Michael was trying to impress upon Chris was **STICK TO YOUR PLAN!** If you reach your goal get out of the casino with the money! Without discipline people start to say, "If I won one hundred seventy-five dollars in twenty minutes, I can win three hundred and fifty dollars in forty minutes!" That line of thinking will get you in trouble! More than likely, you will lose the one hundred seventy-five dollars that you won plus some or all of your original buy-in. When you get greedy, you get burned. Time is your enemy. Spending a lot of time at the tables is extremely dangerous. The casinos know and understand this concept. The casinos will do everything to distract you from your focus. Free booze, attractive ladies, and, of course, comps.

It is important to understand the difference between gambling and gaming! Gambling is where a person is betting a little money to win a lot of money but with a *low probability (low percentage)* of winning, e.g., playing the lottery, betting on the two or twelve on the craps layout, etc. The reason the casinos call it the gaming industry is because they are putting up a large amount of money to make a small return (2 to 7%) (a little bit of money), but with a *high probability* of winning and on *high volume*. For example, slot machines pay out ninety-eight percent. What this actually means is that the casinos are making two percent on every dollar bet. They win no matter what happens. What's 2% of $1,000,000,000 (one billion dollars)? The answer is TWENTY MILLION. Over the course of a month, that's how palatial properties like the Bellagio and Wynn Casinos are built.

This is also true for the poker tables. The casinos take a small percentage of each pot just for the players to have the privilege of being able to play at the poker table. Again, the casino *wins no matter what* the outcome for the other poker players. With craps, they are offering to pay thirty dollars for each one dollar wagered on a two or twelve bet because they have a ninety-seven point two percent (97.2%) probability of winning, meaning the bettor has a less than three percent (3%) chance of winning. Again, the player is betting a little money with the hope of winning a lot of money with a very small chance (low probability) to do so (gambling), whereas the casino is wagering (paying or risking?) a lot of money to win a small amount but with an extremely high chance to do so (gaming). By the way: true odds on a two or twelve are 36 for 1, not 30 for one. There is only one way to roll a Two or Twelve of the 36 combination of numbers on two dice. Once again, the casino wins no matter what, over time.

Michael and Chris stood at the craps table watching. The shooter, a man in his early forties bet twenty-five dollars on the Pass Line. His first roll of the dice was a Six. Michael instructed Chris to take detailed notes. Chris wrote down on his yellow pad under Shooter One; Six. Michael then told Chris if they were going to bet they would bet the "Modified Iron Cross" by betting ten dollars on the Four, twenty-five dollars on the Five, thirty dollars on the Six and Eight each, ten dollars on the Nine and Ten, plus ten dollars in the Field. Chris frantically scratched down the bet. The next roll of the dice was an Eight. Michael instructed Chris to write down net win of twenty-five dollars, replace Field bet. The next roll was a Twelve. Michael told Chris to write down thirty dollar net win, tell dealer to take all bets down or turn them off and remove Field bet plus the profit. The shooter rolled the dice for seven more rolls with various numbers before he rolled a Seven out.

The next shooter was a young woman, probably in her mid to late twenties. She rolled a Seven, a Two and an Eleven before she established a point of Nine. Michael told Chris to write down the same bet as before: ten dollars on the Four, twenty-five dollars on the Five, thirty dollars on the Six and Eight each, ten dollars on the Nine and Ten, plus ten dollars as a Field bet. Chris again frantically wrote down every word that Michael uttered. This served two purposes: one it kept Chris focused on the bets to be made and two, it kept him from being distracted by what other players at the table were doing. The shooter rolled a Four. Michael told Chris to write down, "Win ten dollars on Field bet plus eighteen dollars on the Place bet on the Four."

The next roll of the dice was a Five. Michael told Chris to write down "Win, thirty-five dollars on the Place bet on the Five and loss ten dollar Field bet, a net win of twenty-five dollars. Tell dealer to turn all bets off." The young woman shooter rolled a few more rolls before she Sevened out. Chris wrote down all of the numbers.

Michael turned to Chris and asked him how much they were up. Chris looked at his notes and quickly told Michael that if they had been betting they would be up ninety-eight dollars. Michael next told Chris that at this point in time they would be done and would need to walk away from the table. But Michael wanted to illustrate what could happen on the next shooter. So he told Chris, "Let's see what happens on this next shooter. Remember, we've already made our money on just two shooters and we are done."

The next shooter appeared to be a businessman with some friends. They were drinking, laughing, and being loud. The shooter established a point and within two rolls immediately Sevened out. Michael turned to Chris and said, "Let's go."

Michael found a quiet table in the deli area for him and Chris to talk. "So, Chris, do you see the value of setting a specific, realistic and attainable goal? If you had bet on that third shooter you would have lost all of your profit and then some."

Chris acknowledged that he was starting to understand the concepts Michael was teaching. Michael told Chris there were other types of bets he could make and that he would share them with him the next day. It was late and Michael was tired. Chris admitted he was tired as well and they agreed to call it a night.

Leave the table once you made your goal, no matter how quickly or how you made it.

Chapter SEVEN

Lessons Learned

Chris had an advantage over most people in that he made his home in Las Vegas. He did not need to worry about hotels, airfare or rental cars. He could come and go to any casino any time he pleased and he did not have the extra expense of traveling, e.g., no airfare, parking fees, taxi ride expenses or eating at restaurants. The next morning Chris awoke with a renewed sense of purpose. He drove down to the Gamblers General Store to look for books about craps.

Chris spoke to Mary who had been working for the Gamblers Book Club for more than ten years. The Gamblers Book Club purchased Gamblers General Store. Mary was the gaming book specialist and an expert on the best books about gambling. He asked Mary to recommend a few books about craps. The books recommended by Mary were **Wholly Craps** by David Medansky, **Casino Craps for the Winner** by Avery Cardoza and **The Dice Doctor** by Sam Grafstein. Chris purchased all three books and went back home to begin his reading. He called to confirm with Michael their meeting and mentioned that he was studying.

Later that afternoon they met to begin the next lesson. Michael brought a gift for Chris. It was John Scarne's book, **Scarne on Dice**. Michael explained that, in his opinion, John Scarne was one of the best authors about winning at craps. Michael suggested that they wait a few days to begin the next lesson so that Chris had time to read and absorb the information in the books he had just attained.

Over the course of the next several days, however, Chris met with Michael to watch what was occurring at the craps table.

Michael realized he had to teach Chris to think on his own because he would not be around all of the time to help him. Michael believed in the old biblical adage, "Give a man a fish and he eats for a day. Teach a man to fish and he eats for a lifetime." Michael had Chris take detailed notes of what Chris observed at the table and the two would later discuss what strategy to implement and why.

Another betting method Michael taught Chris was how to bet on the Come out roll without making a Pass Line or Don't Pass Line bet. Michael explained to Chris that he could still participate in the Come out roll action by betting one dollar on the "Yo" (eleven); two dollars on "Any Craps," and two dollars on "Any Seven." This is the 'special' one, two, two, bet. **The total bet was five dollars**.

The rationale for the bet is as follows: Player A bets five dollars on the Pass Line; Player B bets one dollar on the Yo; two dollars on Any Craps and two dollars on Any Seven (A total bet of five dollars). If a Two, Three, or Twelve are rolled, Player A loses his Pass Line bet. Player B, however, is paid eleven dollars (fourteen dollars for the Any Craps bet less the one dollar Yo bet, less the two dollar Any Seven bet and the same bet stays up). If an Eleven is rolled Player A is paid five dollars for his Pass Line bet while Player B is paid eleven dollars net for his combo bet. If a Seven is rolled both Player A and B are each paid five dollars.

Chris, being competitive, chimed in and said, "The flaw in your bet is that if the shooter establishes a point, Player B loses his money and Player A still has his bet."

"Yes," said Michael, "You are absolutely correct, except that we will not know if Player A loses or wins his Pass Line bet until the shooter either makes the point or Sevens out."

Michael said to Chris, "Let me try to explain why the Pass

Line bet is a bad bet. Player A makes a five dollar Pass Line bet and takes odds. If the point is a Four or Ten, he places double odds or ten dollars behind the line. Player A's total bet is fifteen dollars. Now Player B wagers the exact same amount, fifteen dollars on a Place bet on either a Four or Ten depending on which number is the point. If the shooter makes the Four (or Ten if Ten is the point), Player A is paid a total of twenty-five dollars; five dollars even money on his Pass Line bet and twenty dollars for his odds bet. Player B is paid twenty-seven dollars. **So even though Player A and Player B wagered the exact same amount for the exact same outcome, Player B made two dollars more** (thirteen and one third percent more) than Player A. The exact same rationale applies to the Five and Nine. With regard to the Six and Eight, the difference is so small it does not matter, except Player B has total control over his money and Player A does not. Player A cannot remove his Pass Line bet. He can only remove his behind the line odds. Player B, on the other hand, can turn off his Place bet or ask that it be taken down. "

Michael continued, "The beauty of the Place bet is that I have total control over my money. If the shooter has rolled five or six numbers and I am concerned that the Seven will appear, I can ask that my bets be taken down or turned off. The person who makes a Pass Line bet cannot take down or turn off his Pass Line bet. He can only take down his odds."

Chris was amazed at the difference of how a person bet could be the difference between winning and losing. He had never heard of anyone taking down a bet or turning off a bet. If anything, he was taught the opposite – to press winning bets. He was starting to realize why he had been losing money playing craps instead of making money.

Michael continued the lesson. "Another thing that most people do not realize is that most of the time there is a range of three to five shooters, where each will roll at least three numbers after establishing a point before rolling a Seven." Michael explained that knowing this small bit of information is why he only bets on three or four shooters at one session. He told Chris that he has seen where every shooter, at a full table – twelve to thirteen players - would roll at least two numbers after establishing a point before rolling a Seven, but that it was rare. He went on to explain that more often than not a "point Seven out" or "point number Seven" out came in bunches, and that it was better to either not bet or bet on the Don't ("Dark") side.

The session was over because Michael noticed Chris was being overwhelmed with information again. He suggested they meet the next day. Chris agreed. His head was spinning with all of the information Michael was giving him. To say the least, he was overwhelmed.

Michael had a point to make with Chris but was not certain how to broach the subject. He did not want to upset Chris, but was worried that what he might tell him next would for sure upset him. Michael decided just to speak his mind. He said to Chris, "Hey man, I don't want to piss you off or anything but you need to understand something before we go any further." Chris wondered what the heck Michael could be talking about. Chris smiled his famous broad smile as he was open to any suggestion Michael had and said, "No worries. What is it?"

Michael explained that he had an opportunity to hear Joe Montana speak and that Montana had said something that stuck with Michael. It was a philosophy Michael adapted in every aspect of his life. Chris' guard immediately went up hearing the name Joe Montana. Lately, Chris did not like to talk much about football. He certainly did not want to hear about a guy who had been to four Super Bowls and won four rings when he had been to three Super Bowls and never got one ring.

Michael said, "Montana said when he played for the 49ers, they didn't practice until they got the play right. They practiced until they did not get the play wrong." Michael added his own belief about practice, "Most people believe practice makes perfect. It doesn't. That is a myth. Practice only makes habit. Perfect practice makes perfect. If you are not doing it right to begin with then you must keep doing it until you not only get it right, but never get it wrong thereafter." Michael continued, "You know, Chris, I've met people who tell me they have been playing craps for twenty years or more or doing something for a long time. You know what my response to those people is - - that doesn't mean you've been doing it right for all those years."

Chris nodded his head in agreement with Michael. "I get what you're saying, we keep working on this until I don't get it wrong," Chris replied.

Chapter EIGHT

A Rough Start

The sky was majestic blue as Chris drove from his home to the MGM Casino. He was ready to start making some money playing craps. He read the books he purchased about craps and studied his notes. The excitement and anticipation of making money was building inside his body. It was all he could do to control his emotions.

Michael met Chris at the craps table. He was there to observe and correct Chris if needed. Chris bought in for one thousand dollars. He waited patiently as the shooter rolled a few numbers and then a Seven out. The next shooter was passed five dice. He selected two of the die and turned them so that the three was facing on top of each. Chris bet one dollar on the Yo, two dollars on Any Craps and two dollars on Any Seven. The shooter rolled an Eight. Chris lost his five dollar bet. He thought, "Okay, no worries, it is only five dollars."

He had his money ready and instructed the dealer to place ten dollars on the Four, twenty-five dollars on the Five, thirty dollars on the Six, ten dollars on the Nine and Ten. He then put ten dollars in the Field and made a thirty dollar Place bet on the Eight by placing the chips half way on the Pass Line and telling the dealer "Place bet on the Eight." The next roll was an Eleven. Chris was paid ten dollars for his Field bet. The shooter again set the dice and tossed them gently toward the opposite end of the table. As the dice were in the air Chris was thinking "Any number but Seven, any number but Seven." The dice bounced and spun at the other end of the table. One of the die hit a player's chips before settling down. The stick person called out, "Seven out, line away." Chris lost one hundred twenty dollars on that shooter. He had a sick feeling inside his stomach.

He glared at Michael wondering what the hell just happened. It was like someone just punched him the gut. Michael saw the anger in Chris's eyes and told him, "Just wait. Be patient. Do not bet on the next few shooters until I tell you to do so." Chris shook his head and followed Michael's instructions.

The next three shooters all either rolled one or two numbers after establishing a point before they rolled a Seven out. It was a very cold table. The fourth shooter had a decent roll of about six numbers before rolling a Seven. Michael told Chris to bet on the very next shooter. The next shooter's first roll was a Four. The stick person instructed the dealers to mark the Four as the point. Michael told Chris to double his bet. Chris wasn't thrilled with the idea and was a bit nervous. Chris bet twenty dollars on the Four, fifty dollars on the Five, sixty dollars on the Six and Eight each, twenty dollars on the Nine and Ten, plus a twenty dollar Field bet. The shooter tossed the dice as Chris anxiously watched. The stick person called out, "Five, no Field Five." Chris lost his twenty dollar Field bet, but won seventy dollars for his Place bet on the Five, a net win of fifty dollars. He replaced his twenty dollar Field bet.

The shooter was passed the dice again. This time as the dice were in the air, Chris closed his eyes. He could not watch. A cheer went up from the players at his table. Chris opened his eyes as the stick person called out "Four, Hard Four, pay the line." The shooter made his point. Chris was paid twenty dollars for his Field bet and thirty-six dollars for his Place bet on the Four, a net win of fifty-six dollars. Michael told Chris to take his bets down. Chris did as he was instructed. He won back almost everything he lost on the first shooter. Chris reduced his bets to a combined bet of one hundred twenty-five dollars over the next three shooters. He made an average of fifty dollars on each shooter. Michael suggested they stop, as Chris was now ahead one hundred forty dollars. Chris did not argue with Michael.

The two went to the Cashier's Cage where Chris exchanged his chips for legal tender. They found a quiet spot to talk and discuss what just occurred. Michael started the conversation by telling Chris it would take him getting comfortable with losing green chips (twenty-five dollars) before being comfortable betting larger amounts. Chris understood. Money was moderately tight for Chris and he was in no position to "gamble" it away frivolously.

After about half an hour Michael suggested they walk over to New York, New York and play another session. As the two walked, Michael reminded Chris of what they had discussed. When they got on an acceptable table Michael quickly surveyed the layout. There were six players making bets. Two of them had Come bets with odds; the Come bets were on the Six and the Nine. The energy level was decent at the table with several players being in jovial moods as opposed to being down. Michael also noticed that the shooter had most of the numbers on the feature bet called the "All Small and All Tall" marked. This was an indication that the shooter had a good roll. The next roll of the dice was a Seven out.

Chris bought in for one thousand dollars. A new shooter was Coming out. This time Chris did not make his "special" dollar "Yo", two dollar Any Craps and two dollar Any Seven bet. He waited. The shooter's Come-out roll was a Nine. Chris made the standard bet of ten dollars on the Four, twenty-five dollars on the Five, thirty dollars on the Six and Eight each, ten dollars on the Nine and Ten, plus a ten dollar Field bet.

This is how Chris' bet looked:

4	5	6	8	9	10	Field	
$10	$25	$30	$30	$10	$10	$10	= $125 Total

Feeling confident, Chris watched as the shooter tossed the dice. As they glided through the air and landed at the opposite end of the table, they barely hit the back wall and softly settled showing a two and four. The stick person called out, "Six, Six came easy. Hard Six is down." Chris was paid thirty five dollars for his Place bet on the Six. He quickly replaced his ten dollar Field bet. The next roll of the dice was a Four. Chris collected his Field bet and the winnings; was paid eighteen dollars for his Place bet on the Four and asked the dealer to turn off his bets. A few rolls later, the shooter Sevened out.

Chris made the same bet for the next two shooters. Within twenty minutes he was up more than one hundred fifty dollars. Michael instructed Chris to color up. It was time to leave. Chris was having too much fun. He enjoyed making money. He thought, like most people, if I can make one hundred fifty dollars in twenty minutes then I certainly can make three hundred in forty minutes. In reality it does not work that way. Reluctantly he followed Michael's instructions and colored up. Michael said, "Let's head back to the MGM for another session."

At the MGM craps table Michael told Chris they were going to do something different. This was going to be a test for Chris to see if he could exercise self control and discipline. Michael wasn't sure how the test would work out but wanted to give it a try anyway. The shooter was in the middle of a long roll. He eventually rolled an Eleven and then made his point. It became a new Come-out roll. Michael had a hunch and instructed Chris to bet five dollars on the Eleven; ten dollars on Any Craps; and ten dollars on Any Seven; a total of twenty-five dollars. Chris tossed out the bet to the stick person and repeated the bet Michael told him. Chris's bet looked like this:

Yo (Eleven)	Any Craps	Any Seven		
$5	$10	$10	=	$25 Total

The shooter set the dice carefully, banged them on the table and let them fly. The stick person called out, "Two, aces on the faces. Take the Pass Line, pay the Don'ts." The stick person instructed the dealer to pay Chris fifty-five dollars.

Other players replaced their Pass Line bets and a few made Horn bets. The shooter's next roll was a one and a two; the stickperson called out, "Three, craps take the line, pay the Field." Chris was paid another fifty-five dollars. The next roll was an Eleven. The table cheered. Chris was paid another fifty-five dollars. So far he was up one hundred sixty-five dollars for his twenty-five dollar 'Special" bet. The next roll was an Eight. Chris lost his twenty-five dollar bet but overall was still up one hundred forty dollars. Michael instructed Chris to color up. Chris was wide eyed. They just got to the table. They only bet on one shooter. Michael was nuts, he thought.

Chris exchanged his chips for cash at the Cashier's Cage and joined Michael who was waiting for him at the sports bar deli nearby. "Okay Michael, why did we leave that table so soon?" Chris asked. Michael was tired and quietly asked Chris, "How much did you just make on the one shooter?"

"One hundred and forty dollars."

"And how much are you up so far for today?"

"About four hundred and thirty dollars," Chris said nonchalantly.

"And your goal was to make four hundred fifty for the day?"

"Yeah, so what's your point?"

"You're close enough; you're about ninety-six percent of your goal. Time to stop for the day."

Chris said, "Okay, I see what you're saying. Man, this is hard. We just got started and it seems like we're done already."

Michael chuckled. "I told you it was simple, just not easy to execute. How do you think people who travel to Vegas feel? They spend all of that time and money to get here and then they get to the craps table. They make their money quickly and then what are they going to do? Sit in their room? Unlikely! So they stay at the table longer and most of them will end up losing. They came to Vegas to gamble and so they did. You on the other hand can go home and carry on with normal life."

"Tomorrow where do you want to play?" Michael asked Chris. Chris said he wanted to meet at the Orleans, as it was one of his favorite places off the Strip to play.

Chapter NINE

Every Master has had at least one disaster!

An ominous omen filled the air as Michael approached Chris who was already standing at the craps table. Chris had bought in and was in the middle of playing when Michael took the spot next to him. "How's it going?" Michael asked.

"So far so good," Chris replied. "This is the second shooter I made bets. I'm up seventy-five dollars so far."

"Excellent!" Michael responded.

The shooter's next roll was a Six. Chris was paid and asked the dealer to take down his bets. Michael was impressed that Chris turned off his bets as he was supposed to do. The shooter continued with rolling number after number. About ten more numbers after Chris had taken down his bets he got anxious. He could not control himself. He thought this was a hot shooter. He could make all of his money for the day on this shooter alone.

Chris asked the dealer to turn his bets back on again. Michael did not say a word. He watched to see what would happen. The shooter rolled another six rolls. It was a great roll. The players at the table were all cheering and hollering after each toss of the dice.

By now, Chris was up another three hundred dollars. He kept playing. Instead of taking his winning payouts he started to press his bets. Not only did he press his bets he started to make bets on all of the hard-way numbers. A few more rolls later the shooter finally rolled a Seven out. All in all, Chris was still up more than three hundred dollars. He was all smiles.

The next shooter established a point of Ten. Before Michael had a chance to say anything Chris made a large total combined bet for the "Modified Iron Cross." He bet twenty dollars on the Four, fifty dollars on the Five, sixty dollars on the Six and Eight each, twenty dollars on the Nine and Ten; plus a twenty dollar Field bet. He had two hundred fifty dollars on the layout. Being the natural competitor, Chris also bet twenty-five dollars on each of the hard-way numbers. Chris turned to Michael, smiled and said, "Watch and learn.

Michael was shocked that Chris would bet so much at one time. He had not had the opportunity to teach Chris that usually after a hot shooter, the table can turn quickly and the next few shooters generally have short rolls. Michael prayed he would be wrong this time.

The shooter was an attractive young lady in her mid-twenties. She wore a low cut dress that revealed a lot. Her boyfriend stood next to her as she picked up the dice. She tossed them in the air toward the other end of the table. Each die spun around on the green felt, hit a few of the chips on the layout and settled showing a three and a four. The stick person called out, "Seven out, line away." The dealers' hands moved quickly collecting all of the chips and locking them up in the table's bank.

Chris had a horrified look on his face. He just lost three hundred fifty dollars. Now, instead of being up, he was actually down. He quickly colored up his chips and left the table. Michael followed a close distance behind him. Once they reached a spot to talk, Chris started in on Michael about how his method does not work; that he could have made a killing on the hot shooter if it weren't for Michael's method of play. Michael waited until Chris was finished. "Are you done?" He asked. Chris responded, "Yes." He was starting to cool down.

"Let's review what happened. First of all, you violated all of the rules. You made your goal for the day on one shooter and did not stop. There was no reason to bet on that young lady. There's a lot to learn about the trends of a craps table. Quite often, after a hot roll, the next shooter will have a very short roll. You just witnessed this for yourself. The second mistake was to press up your bets. You pressed the Modified Iron Cross to two hundred fifty dollars and made one hundred dollars in prop bets (twenty-five dollars each on all the hard ways). Third mistake, you simply got caught up in the excitement of the game. What did we discuss about perfect practice makes perfect the other day?" Chris realized that he had blamed Michael when the truth of the matter was he was mad at himself. He knew it was his fault.

Michael suggested that they not play anymore that day. Michael told Chris, "It is not good to be playing craps when you are upset. A negative mind will never give you a positive life." Chris did not want to stop he wanted to try to recoup his loss and make the goal of four hundred fifty dollars. Michael reluctantly agreed. They went back to the craps table.

Michael could tell from the chips on the layout and the low energy of the players this was not going to end well. Again he suggested to Chris not to play anymore. Chris was confident he could follow the rules.

The first player Chris bet on immediately established a point and then rolled a Seven out. Chris waited until the table was re-qualified. He waited until a shooter rolled at least three box numbers after a point was established. Michael suggested they wait for two shooters to roll at least three box numbers after establishing a point. Chris followed Michael's instructions. Unfortunately, the shooter that Chris made his bet rolled a point and then a Seven out. Finally, Chris decided it was time to stop.

Michael could tell Chris was agitated by what just happened. It was a loss, but nothing significant in the grand scheme of life. Michael attempted to comfort Chris by explaining that there will be days when nothing you do will work out. There will be those days when nothing you do will be right and you will lose money. It happens. That's why they call it gambling. Michael put it in football terms. He explained to Chris that you can call the perfect play, and it can be executed perfectly, but the other team still makes great play to stop you. Chalk it up to great defense and get back to the huddle.

Michael further told Chris that before he got real good at making money playing craps it took a lot of work, frustration and losing money before he started to make money. As Michael put it to Chris, "Malcolm Gladwell in his book, Outlier, states that it takes more than ten thousand hours to master a skill, craft or trade." Chris had put his ten thousand hours in before, playing in the NFL. And while he might have played more than ten thousand hours at the craps table, he was not playing correctly to make money.

"Chris, there is still tomorrow to start fresh. You can still make the ten thousand dollars in a month if you will let me finish teaching you. We have only scratched the surface. You need to master the first level before moving to the next level." Chris was in a better mood and agreed to continue with the lesson before playing without Michael's help again.

Once you understand and accept that you can never be flawless in the game of craps, you will become less frustrated by the few bad days you may have losing money.

Michael wanted to emphasize to Chris the importance of why he only made one or two bets per shooter and then took his bets down or turned them off. "The analogy I use as to why I take my bets down or turn them off within one or two rolls after a shooter establishes a point is compared to playing poker. In poker you do not play every hand dealt. Most successful poker players fold early in the hand to either avoid paying the ante or to avoid losing a lot. So while the poker player may have folded a 'winning' hand, they do so to minimize their risk of losing. It cost nothing to watch."

"Similarly, in craps, I remove my bets early in a shooter's roll to minimize my risk. While I may miss out on a 'hot' shooter, I also avoid losing on the 'cold' and 'choppy' shooters."

Volatility is to be expected.
Do not be discouraged by a few rough days.

Michael wanted to talk with Chris about focus, fear and greed. He started the conversation by stating quoting Robert Kiyosaki, who said, "The main reason most people are not rich is because they are terrified of losing. Winners are not afraid of losing. But losers are. Failure is part of the process of success. People who avoid failure also avoid success."

Michael continued and asked if Chris had ever heard of Dave Ramsey? Chris replied that he did. "Excellent!" Michael said. He continued, "Dave Ramsey, in his great book, **Entreleadership,** writes about focus and fear. Mr. Ramsey related the story of asking an NFL veteran wide receiver "How is it that you get paid tem million dollars a year to one thing, catch a football, and then sometimes you drop it?" The veteran NFL player did not realize Mr. Ramsey was being facetious when he asked the question. He truthfully answered that there are two primary reasons a professional player loses focus and drops the football. The first reason a player loses focus is fear. The same applies to a craps player. Fear of losing money will cause a player to lose focus every time. Fear of losing causes a player to fixate on the potential for failure instead of concentrating on success. The player explained to Mr. Ramsey

"When a 310 pound man is chasing you with world-class speed, you literally hear footsteps that signal huge amounts of pain to follow. That signal of impending pain generates actual fear, which can cause you to lose focus and drop the ball, even if are paid ten million dollars to do one thing: catch a football."[1]

The player further told Mr. Ramsey the second reason a wide receiver loses focus is greed. In the case of a football player he looks at the end zone *before* catching the ball. In his mind he sees himself scoring before he actually catches the football. When the player turns to catch the ball he fails to watch the ball go into his hands because he has focused on scoring. When the ball arrives, it is too late and he misses. Chris interjected, "Yeah, I can relate to what that player is saying. But how does that apply to winning at craps?"

Michael answered, "Craps players are no different. When a craps player gets greedy he loses focus on achieving his goal and lets his chips remain on the table too long; or worse, increases his bets. You experienced that yourself today. Need I say more?"

Chris understood exactly what Michael was saying to him. "No, I get it."

Michael was not so sure that Chris understood the lesson.

---

[1] *Entreleadership* by Dave Ramsey, page 83-84, Howard Books 2011

He wanted to really drive the point home. "Chris, let's look at it from a different approach. The Universe will give you what you want so long as you are very specific. Think of it as a drive thru window at a fast food chain, like McDonald's. When you go through the drive through window you are very clear on your order. You tell the person taking the order exactly what you want. Then you go to the next window and pay for your food. You make an exchange. You then receive your order and enjoy it. Wouldn't you say that is very simple?"

"So how does that apply to craps you might be thinking? It is very simple. You set a goal, i.e., you tell the Universe exactly how much you want to win for the day. You then take action by playing – you put in the time and effort (an exchange). You then collect your winnings and enjoy."

"Are you going to win every time? Of course not! Just like the drive through can make a mistake with your order, the Universe will not grant your wish every day. Today, you won the amount you set as your goal very quickly. The Universe granted your wish. But by continuing to play you gave mixed signals to the Universe. When you are not very specific with what you want, you sometimes get something different. Sometimes you will win more; more often than not you will lose. In any event, the lesson is that if you give mixed messages to the Universe you won't know what to expect. We have talked about setting Specific, Measurable, Attainable, Realistic and Timely goals. S.M.A.R.T. goals."

Chris left with a lot to think about. Michael had presented information in a new way to think about everything. Had he stopped after achieving his goal he would have not lost money on the other shooters. Chris was starting to understand why it is so difficult to win consistently. He kept changing his mind as to what he wanted. He now understood what Michael was trying to teach him. Just because you make three hundred dollars in an hour does not mean you will make six hundred dollars in two hours. It was the setting of the goals that gave the specific instructions to the Universe. Changing the goal amount in mid-stream was like changing your order three or four times at the drive thru window. There was bound to be a mistake made. There was too much confusion as to what being asked to be given.

UNCERTAINTY

Every aspect in life is about uncertainty. There are no guarantees. It is how you deal with uncertainty that determines if you succeed or not. All you can do is prepare, do your best and deal with the outcome. No matter who you are or how good you are you can never be perfect playing craps. There is a lot of uncertainty in the game. You must be emotionally, psychologically and mentally ready to deal with the uncertainty of the game. If you are not, it will chew you up and spit you out.

Chapter TEN
Back to Basics

The sunrise was awesome on a gorgeous day. Michael met Chris at a local diner, Blueberry Hill, on Flamingo Avenue, just east of the Strip. He thought it would be a better atmosphere to talk with Chris about making money playing craps. They ordered breakfast and Michael began by recapping what he had previously taught Chris. Chris took out his handy dandy notebook and began taking notes.

1. Making a "Modified Iron Cross" bet of ten dollars on the Four, twenty-five dollars on the Five, thirty dollars on the Six and Eight, ten dollars on the Nine and Ten, plus a ten dollar Field bet was a total combined bet of one hundred twenty-five dollars.

2. Wait until after a shooter establishes a point before making the bet. If the shooter rolls several Sevens, Twos, Three's Elevens or Twelve on the Come Out roll before establishing a point **DO NOT BET on this shooter.** More likely than not, based on my experience, the shooter will immediately Seven out after establishing a point.

3. The average win per roll is twenty-five dollars. Betting just two rolls per shooter equals fifty dollars per shooter. Three shooters at fifty dollars average per shooter equal one hundred fifty dollars per session. Three sessions per day equals four hundred fifty dollars per day. Twenty days per month times four hundred fifty dollars equals nine thousand dollars per month. Nine thousand dollars per month times twelve months per year equals one hundred eight thousand dollars per year.

4. Generally, there will be three to five shooters on average who will roll more than three numbers before a Seven out before you start seeing shooters establishing a point and then Seven out, or establishing a point, roll a number, and then Seven out.

5. If a shooter establishes a number and immediately rolls a Seven out or a number and then a Seven out **DO NOT BET** on the next few shooters until you re-qualify the table. To re-qualify a table wait for a shooter (two shooters if you want to be ultra conservative) to roll three box numbers after establishing a point. Then bet on the next shooter.

6. If you have a loss on a point Seven out or point number Seven out, double the bet size for two rolls after the table is re-qualified. Then reduce bet to normal amount.

7. Once you win your goal amount or are very close to the amount, *immediately leave the table and end the session!*

Chris asked about the one, two, two "Special" Come-out roll bet. Michael suggested that Chris focus just on the "Modified Iron Cross" bet and to master that betting technique before learning other bets. Chris was a bit insulted. Michael did not care about Chris' feelings. He wanted to help Chris earn money at the craps table.

Chris pondered what Michael had told him and then asked, "What about playing the 'Don't' side when the table is cold?" Michael explained to Chris that it was sometimes risky to do this inasmuch as a shooter might roll a Seven or an Eleven on the Come-out roll before establishing a point. If that happened then the "Don't" Pass Line bettors would lose. He went on to tell Chris of how one shooter rolled either a Seven or an Eleven five times in a row and that he lost a lot of money being stubborn.

Not wanting to let the issue alone, Chris pressed Michael for more information. "Okay, so how do you bet if the table is very cold or choppy?" He asked. Michael replied, "On the Come-out roll I 'lay' all of the box numbers for thirty dollars each and bet five dollars on a Horn high 'Yo.' Although I have to put up one hundred eighty-five dollars, I only have thirty-five dollars at risk." Chris looked puzzled. "What do you mean you only have thirty-five dollars at risk?" He asked.

"Simple," Michael said. "I can only lose on one box number at a time plus the five dollar Horn high 'Yo' bet. Let's say the shooter rolls a Six on the Come-out roll, I lose my thirty dollar lay bet on the Six plus the Horn bet, a total of thirty-five dollars. The other lay bets are not affected. But if the shooter rolls a Two, Three, Eleven or Twelve, my lay bets are not affected and I win on the Horn high 'Yo' bet. If the shooter rolls a Seven, I win all of my lay bets, less the vig (one dollar each; six dollars in total) and lose my Horn hi 'Yo' bet. So I would win one hundred twenty dollars, less the five dollar Horn hi 'Yo' bet less the six dollar vig, a net total of one hundred nine dollars. Not a bad ratio of risking thirty-five dollars to win about one hundred ten dollars."

Chris was still confused by what Michael had just told him. He sat scratching his head trying to understand how Michael would win one hundred twenty dollars on his lay bet of one hundred eighty dollars. Michael could see that Chris did not understand what he was talking about. "Do you know the proper payouts on a lay bet?" Michael asked.

"No I don't," Chris said.

"Do you even know what a lay bet is?" Michael asked.

"Yeah, I do. It is where you make a bet that a Seven will appear before a specific box number. Most people will lay the Four and Ten because they only have three ways to lose and six ways to win on a Seven. Any other number does not affect the lay bet."

"Absolutely" Michael said. "The risk with a lay bet is that you must bet more money to win less because the probability is on the bettor's side. So in my bet of laying the numbers for thirty dollars each, plus a one dollar vig, I will win a different amount on each number if a Seven is rolled. The Four and Ten will pay fifteen dollars each (I bet two dollars to make one dollar, a 2 to 1 ratio); the Five and Nine will pay twenty dollars each (I bet three dollars to make two dollars, a 3 to 2 ratio); and I make twenty-five dollars on the Six and Eight each (I bet six dollars to make five dollars, a 6 to 5 ratio)."

Michael continued his explanation, "The problem with most craps players is that they do not understand the math behind the bets. They have not taken the time to learn why certain bets are paid a certain way. With a lay bet on the Four there are only three ways to make a Four; a three and one, a one and three; and a two and two. But there are six ways to make a Seven: a one and six; a six and one; a two and five; a five and two; a three and four; and a four and three. Hence, six ways to win verses three ways to lose, six to three is the same as two to one. That is why a person takes odds on a Pass Line bet if the point is Four, they are paid two to one. The same applies to the Ten. The casinos are smart and they don't want a player to have any advantage. So they charge you a vig (commission) to make that bet. Their game, their rules."

Chris was beginning to see why understanding the math behind the game was so important.

Michael paid the check and the two headed to the Luxor.

At ten o'clock in the morning only one craps table was open. There were six people standing at the table. Only four, however, were actually playing. The other two were watching the action. Chris bought in for one thousand dollars. He followed Michael's one betting method of the "Modified Iron Cross" for a total combined bet of one hundred twenty-five dollars. He averaged fifty dollars on each shooter and only bet on three shooters. He cashed out with one thousand one hundred fifty dollars.

Michael suggested they go to the Bellagio to play. He wanted to get Chris use to leaving a casino quickly. At the Bellagio, Chris won another one hundred fifty dollars within twenty minutes. The next stop was Bally's. Again, Chris made one hundred fifty dollars quickly. It was an ideal table where each shooter rolled four or five numbers after establishing a point before a Seven out. There were no hot shooters with long rolls. They headed back to get Chris's car at Blueberry Hill.

While at the diner, they stopped in for a cup of coffee to review the day's action. Michael began the conversation, "Sometimes people, me included, over think things; we out smart ourselves. Today is a perfect example of what I'm talking about. You bought in for one thousand dollars and made on average one hundred fifty dollars each session. That is fifteen percent. Most people would be ecstatic to make fifteen percent interest on their money in a year let alone in less than an hour. But the beauty of all this is that by playing three sessions you won four hundred fifty dollars with the same one thousand dollar buy-in. So in reality you made forty-five percent on your money in one day. I can teach you other betting methods and other patterns, but why? What good would it do you? The three simple betting methods you learned are sufficient. So even though there are many more betting methods I can teach, there is no reason to do so. Sometimes I think I know too much and when I try implementing everything at once, I usually end up losing. It always come down to this one thing, I call it the K.I.S.S. rule – Keep It Super Simple."

Chris was actually amazed at the simplicity of Michael's betting method. Yet, he knew, just as Michael had told him, it was difficult to implement. Still if he just followed Michael's rules he would be able to win money consistently. He started to understand the power of keeping it simple. Keeping to the basics and sound fundamentals worked consistently in the NFL. Playing craps should be no different. No matter how many championships they won, no matter how many veteran all pro players he had on the team, Vince Lombardi would begin each season on the first day of practice holding a football in front of the team and he would say, "Gentlemen, this is a football."

Michael gave Chris one more bit of advice. "If you do lay all of the numbers for thirty dollars each, and you make the one hundred nine dollars net, only do it twice. You will make your goal and then some. Also, if you lose thirty five dollars because the shooter rolled a box number, do **NOT** leave your bets up for more than two losses. If you lose seventy dollars, stop."

The next morning Chris received a text message from Michael. The message said that he was traveling to the Caribbean to meet some friends for vacation. Michael wished Chris luck and asked him to keep in touch.

During the next several weeks Chris maintained his self control and discipline. Implementing the simple betting methods he learned from Michael he was able to earn more than ten thousand dollars. Chris played ultra conservatively. When the table conditions were right he bet the Modified Iron Cross. When the table was cold and many shooters were establishing a point and then rolling a Seven out or a number and then a Seven out he laid all of the numbers, plus a Horn high "Yo" bet. Very rarely, and only when he noticed that the shooters were rolling a Seven or Horn number on a Come-out roll did he implement the "Special" one, two, two bet. Just using these three simple methods earned him a lot of money.

Chris was able to donate more than twenty thousand dollars to his foundation *My Fig 8* to support inner-city at risk kids.

> "Mastery is impossible to realize fully. You can hone in on it. You can get really, really, really, close, but never touch it. Great athletes often say they can - - they must get better. What the great athletes understand about mastery is that they will never get it. It will always hover beyond their grasp."
> - - Malcom Gladwell
>
> In his book *Outliers*, author Malcolm Gladwell says that it takes roughly ten thousand hours of practice to achieve mastery in a field.

Chapter ELEVEN

A Negative Mind Will Never give you a Positive Life.

Chris contemplated what he had learned from Michael Caldwell and his chance encounter. He remembered hearing someone tell him, "Some people come into your life for a reason. Others come for a season. Some people come into your life as blessings. Others come into your life as lessons." Michael came into his life for a brief moment. His short encounter certainly left a lifelong impression on Chris. He would never be the same.

The authors are **NOT** recommending, suggesting nor advising that you run out and quit your day job and take-up playing craps full time. Playing craps does not come with medical benefits or any type of guarantee - so do not quit your day job.

The extra money can and does make life nicer and easier. Imagine what an extra two hundred dollars per week can do for you? Remember there will be days when you will have a negative pay check - because you CANNOT win all of the time – no one does. If they tell you they do they are lying. There will be bad days with the good days, limiting your losses will be the keys to your success. Below are several "Lessons" to help you with your craps endeavors.

LESSON ONE: DISCIPLINE

Discipline comes through self-control. This means that one must control all negative qualities. Before you can control conditions, you must first control yourself. Self-mastery is the hardest job you will ever tackle. If you do not conquer self, you will be conquered by self. You may see at the same time both your best friend and your greatest enemy by stepping in front of a mirror. Worrying won't stop the bad stuff from happening it just stops you from enjoying the good things in life.

LESSON TWO: GOALS

Set a *specific, measurable, attainable* and *realistic* goal within a set *time* parameter of how much you want to win and once you make that goal stop. *Leave the table once you've made your goal no matter how quickly or how you made it.*

LESSON THREE: PROBABILITY VS. REALITY

If the probability models worked in the short run as in the long run, the casinos would have been out of business a long time ago. There would be no challenge because we would already know the outcome based on the probability models working in the short run as they do over the long run, i.e., an infinite period of time. Casinos rely on the disproportionate occurrences (streaks) during shorter periods of time when gamblers play (a shorter period of time, in our opinion, is anything less than twenty-four hours straight). The casinos operate twenty-four hours per day, seven days per week, fifty two weeks per year, year after year after year. A person cannot properly function at the tables for more than a few hours.

LESSON FOUR: BANKROLL

You should only play with money you can afford to risk and to make certain you have enough of a bankroll/buy-in to be able to reach a specific, measurable, attainable and realistic goal within a set time period.

LESSON FIVE: SUPERIORITY

To achieve success, you must have superiority. Superiority, however, is relative. *To accomplish superiority over the casino it is only necessary to understand that you do not need to make a wager on every shooter and every roll of the dice. You have the right to be selective as to how much and when to bet.*

LESSON SIX: POINT SEVEN OUT (PSO)
The biggest concern Michael heard from students and other craps player was how to handle the dreaded point Seven out (PSO). Students will ask, "How do I avoid the point Seven out?" Or, "Michael, I lost because of several point Seven outs - - your methods don't work." This is what Michael tells people who are losing because of the point "Seven out" or "point number Seven out." "There is nothing you can do to avoid it. If he had the secret to playing craps and avoiding the point Seven out or point number Seven out, he would be on his yacht in the Caribbean." *Michael told Chris several times that there is no one betting method that works all of the time. There is no magic formula for winning every time. Losses do happen!* It is what you do when you experience a loss or losing session that can make the difference in your mind set and bankroll to make playing craps profitable.

Here is how Michael handles a point Seven out or a point number Seven out. He does *not* bet on the next few shooters. *He waits to qualify a shooter before betting* and then doubles his bet for two rolls. This has been mentioned previously in this book. It is a lesson Michael's students have overlooked or forgotten in the past, so it is being repeated..

LESSON SEVEN: KNOW YOUR LIMITS
Without self discipline, you cannot successfully play craps. You must know when to "walk away" from the craps table to be successful. You cannot and will not succeed if you play continuously. In craps, like most other types of gambling, you do

not increase your winnings by playing longer; you increase your winnings by making larger bets. It does not matter if you play for ten minutes or three hours. The only thing that matters is leaving the craps table with more money than you started with. If you do have a bad start with the dice, walk away and cut your losses. Have a pre-determined amount of money that you are willing to lose. Be certain it is realistic to the size of your bankroll. In the words of Dirty Harry, "A Man has got to know his limits."

Discipline comes through self-control. This means that one must control all negative qualities. Before you can control conditions, you must first control yourself. Self-mastery is the hardest job you will ever tackle. If you do not conquer self, you will be conquered by self. You may see at the same time both your best friend and your greatest enemy by stepping in front of a mirror.

Chapter TWELVE
One Year Later
So you wanna be a High Roller

During the next twelve months Chris had made more than one hundred thousand dollars at the craps table. Life was good. He had not seen nor heard from Michael Caldwell during the past year. It was exactly one year to the day since he first met Caldwell. He decided to go to the Wynn Casino that particular day to reminisce and play some craps.

Chris stood at the craps table and had just made his buy-in. Standing at the opposite end of the table was Michael Caldwell. What a pleasant surprise Chris thought. Caldwell did not notice Chris at the other end of the table. Chris watched Michael to see if he was doing what he taught Chris.

The shooter's Come-out roll was a Nine. Michael bet one hundred dollars on the Four, Nine and Ten; two hundred fifty dollars on the Five; three hundred dollars on the Six and Eight each and made a Field bet of one hundred dollars; a total of one thousand two hundred fifty dollars. His bet looked like this:

4	5	6	8	9	10	Field
$100	$250	$300	$300	$100	$100	$100 = $1,250

Chris was shocked to see such a large bet made by Michael. The shooter picked up the dice and tossed them to the opposite side of the table. They spun around and danced on the felt before settling down. The stick person called out "Eight, Hard Eight." The next roll of the dice was a Four. In two rolls of the dice Michael had made five hundred and thirty dollars. He told the dealer to take all of his bets down. Chris watched as Michael did the same bet for the next two shooters. Chris mimicked Michael's bet, except he was still betting one hundred twenty-five dollars on each roll of the dice.

Michael colored up and saw Chris at the other end of the table smiling at him. Chris colored up too. They met at the Cashier's Cage. "Michael, how are you? Good to see you. Do you have time to have a beer with me?" Chris asked. Michael was in a very good mood and was thrilled to see Chris again.

They sat in the sport's lounge and talked. Chris began the conversation by asking Michael why he was making such a large bet. Michael chuckled and told Chris that this was now his normal bet. Over the years Michael had accumulated enough money to have a substantially large bank roll. Although he would not tell Chris exactly how large he did tell him it was more than two hundred fifty grand. All of it set aside just for craps.

"Chris, I buy-in for ten thousand dollars. The "Modified Iron Cross" bet is twelve and one-half percent of the buy-in. I average two hundred fifty dollars per roll. I only stay up for two rolls per shooter. I make an average of about five hundred dollars per shooter. I only bet on three shooters, unless of course I have a loss. My goal is to make fifteen hundred per session. I play between two and three sessions per day depending on how I feel and how the dice appear to roll. By doing this I will average more than three thousand per day. I only play twenty days each month, sometimes less." Chris did a quick calculation in his head and realized Michael was earning sixty thousand dollars per month.

"Michael, are you telling me you make more than three quarters of a million dollars a year at craps?"

"Maybe; who said I play craps for an entire year?"

Chris laughed. "Still think I work for the IRS?"

Michael invited Chris to dinner that evening. They were

going to go to Aureole Restaurant. It was one of the top ten restaurants in Vegas.

As Chris departed from the sports bar he stopped by the craps table to watch. While he stood there he noticed people buying in for one hundred thousand dollars. He saw players betting with purple, five hundred dollar chips), yellow one thousand dollar chips and white five thousand dollar chips. He thought about Michael betting one thousand two hundred fifty dollars on a single roll of the dice and realized that in the grand scheme of Las Vegas, it was a small amount. As Michael put it, it was all relative to a person's comfort level.

Michael and Chris enjoyed their meal at Aureole. After dinner Michael handed Chris an envelope containing a hand-written letter. Michael asked Chris to read the letter later when he was alone.

The letter read:

Walt Disney said, "If you can dream it . . . you can do it." Absolute faith removes all fear! Napoleon Hill in "Think and Grow Rich" said, "Success equals a focused mind plus a determined heart plus a focused determined team. To be single mindedly focused means refusing to be distracted by anything. First do not be distracted by critical voices in your head. Second, do not be distracted by the critical voices screaming in the minds of many people around you. Your dreams must be more real than your fears." Be courageous, outrageous, and extraordinary! Absolute faith removes all fear! I trust in the dice, therefore they are faithful. I believe in myself and my ability to earn significant amounts of money playing craps. Therefore, I do. Welcome to the team.

MICHAEL CALDWELL'S RECIPE
FOR MAKING MONEY PLAYING CRAPS:

When people think of success and wealth, they think in terms of a formula, a method, or a blueprint. They rarely think in terms of a recipe. Basic formulas generally list the steps or principles to achieve wealth, but in no particular order or intensity. A recipe, on the other hand, is much more precise. It will list the specific ingredients, the exact proportions and the correct sequence for a specific time period. This is an idea – It is one thing to talk about it, it is another thing to go out and **PROVE IT!** Fair warning – this recipe is easy to understand and follow, but almost impossible to execute. In addition, when you are playing with real money and not just practicing, you will have a different psychological experience. Trust us we know. There is a reason we suggest having a large bankroll in proportion to the bet size. If you think you are different and you think you can make the bets set forth below with a small bankroll; well we'll see. Betting with actual money in a casino is not fiction. It is reality.

[Month 1 and Month 2]
<u>LEVEL I</u>

Your Bankroll should be a minimum of $5,000 to withstand losses. Your Buy-in should be a minimum of $1,500 in case of a point Seven out or point number Seven out.

The bet is: Ten dollars on the Four, Nine, Ten and Field; twenty-five dollars on the Five; and thirty dollars on the Six and Eight each.

4	5	6	8	9	10	Field
$10	$25	$30	$30	$10	$10	$10 = $125

Bet just two (2) rolls per shooter **AFTER** the point is established. Based on the bet above you will win an average of twenty-five ($25) dollars per roll. Twenty-five dollars per roll time's two (2) rolls per shooter equal fifty dollars ($50) per shooter. Fifty dollars per shooter time's two[2] (2) shooters per session equal one hundred dollars ($100) per session. One hundred dollars per session times three (3) sessions per day equal three hundred dollars ($300) per day. Three hundred dollars per day times ten (10) days per month equal three thousand dollars ($3,000) per month.

$25/roll X 2 rolls per shooter = $50 per shooter X 2 shooters per session = $100 per session X 3 sessions per day = $300 per day X 10 days per month = $3,000 per month.

You should **STOP** for the day if you lose more than $875 at any one session.*

---

[2] Why two shooters per session? Because on average there will be a range between three to five shooters that will roll at least two numbers after establishing a point before another shooter will roll a point seven out or a point number seven out. This is a similar concept to why we only bet on two rolls after a shooter establishes a point. Based on statistics the *average* shooter will have a decision within 3.37 rolls after establishing a point. We are ultra conservative. We want to remove our bets *before* a seven out. As we have often said, if we are wrong, it costs us nothing to watch. If we are right, we avoid losing a lot of money. The other analogy I use as to why I take my bets down or turn them off within one or two rolls after a shooter establishes a point is compared to playing poker. **In poker you do not play every hand dealt**. Most successful poker players fold early in the hand to either avoid paying the ante or to avoid losing a lot. So while the poker player may have folded a "winning" hand, they do so to minimize their risk of losing. It cost nothing to watch. Similarly, in craps, I do not bet on every shooter's roll so I can minimize my risk. While I may miss out on a 'hot' shooter, I also avoid losing on the 'cold' and 'choppy' shooters; those that will establish a point and then immediately seven out or establish a point, roll a number, and then seven out.

*Lose $125 on PSO; (double bet) + $250 (lose again) + $500 (lose again) = $875 total loss. If you want to be ultra conservative then do not double the bet. Keep it at $125 total combined bet. The reason being that it would only take an additional session (two shooters plus one additional roll) to make up for one loss.

At the end of month one you should now have won $3,000. **Add this to your initial bankroll. Do NOT spend it or use it for any other purpose!** Your bankroll should now be $8,000 ($5,000 + $3,000 = $8,000).

Repeat the same procedure for month two. At the end of month two you should have won another $3,000. **Add this to your initial bankroll. Do NOT spend it or use it for any other purpose! Your bankroll should now be $11,000** ($5,000 + $3,000 + $3,000 = ($11,000).

[Month 3 and Month 4]
LEVEL II

Your Bankroll should be a minimum of $10,000 to withstand losses. If you played for ten days in month one and month two, you should have won an average of $3,000 per month; a total of $6,000. Including a portion of your initial bankroll, you should now have at least a $10,000 bankroll. Your Buy-in should be a minimum of $2,500 in case of a point, Seven out or point, number, Seven out. You should **STOP** for the day if you lose more than $1,900 at any one session.*

The bet is: Ten dollars on the Four, Nine, and Ten, fifty dollars on the Five; and sixty dollars on the Six and Eight each; plus twenty-five dollars in the Field.

4	5	6	8	9	10	Field
$10	$50	$60	$60	$10	$10	$25 = $225

"You must be locked in mentally to win. Be a Craps Robot!"

Bet just two (2) rolls per shooter **AFTER** the point is established. Based on the bet above you will win an average of forty-three ($43) dollars per roll. Forty-three dollars per roll time's two (2) rolls per shooter equal ninety dollars ($86) per shooter. Eighty-six dollars per shooter time's two (2) shooters per session equal one hundred and seventy-two dollars ($172) per session. One hundred and seventy-two dollars per session times three (3) sessions per day equal five hundred and sixteen dollars ($516) per day. Five hundred and sixteen dollars per day times ten (10) days per month equal five thousand one hundred and sixty dollars ($5,160) per month.

$43/roll X 2 rolls per shooter = $86 per shooter X 2 shooters per session = $172 per session X 3 sessions per day = $516 per day X 10 days per month = $5,160 per month.

*Lose $225 on PSO, double bet to $450. Lose again, double bet to $900. Lose again, STOP!!!! $225 + $450 + $900 = $1,575. If you want to be ultra conservative then do not double the bet. Keep it at $225 total combined bet. The reason being that it would only take an additional session (two shooters plus one additional roll) to make up for one loss.

At the end of month three you should have won another $5,160. **Add this to your initial bankroll. Do NOT spend it or use it for any other purpose!** Your bankroll should now be $16,160. ($5,000 + $3,000 + $3,000 + $5,160 = $16,160).

Repeat the same procedure for month four. At the end of month four you should have won another $5,400. **Add this to your bankroll. Do NOT spend it or use it for any other purpose! Your bankroll should now be $21,800.** ($5,000 + $3,000 + $3,000 + $5,160 + $5,160 = $21,320).

[Month 5, Month 6, and Month 7]
LEVEL III

Your Bankroll should be a minimum of $20,000 to withstand losses. Your Buy-in should be a minimum of $5,000 in case of a point Seven out or point number Seven out.

The bet is: Fifty dollars on the Four, Nine, Ten and Field; one hundred twenty-five dollars on the Five; and one hundred fifty dollars on the Six and Eight each.

4	5	6	8	9	10	Field
$50	$125	$150	$150	$50	$50	$50 = $625[3]

Bet just two (2) rolls per shooter **AFTER** the point is established. Based on the bet above you will win an average of one hundred twenty-five ($125) dollars per roll. One hundred twenty-five dollars per roll time's two (2) rolls per shooter equal two hundred fifty dollars ($250) per shooter. Two hundred fifty dollars per shooter time's two (2) shooters per session equal five hundred dollars ($500) per session. Five hundred dollars per session times three (3) sessions per day equal one thousand five hundred dollars ($1,500) per day. One thousand five hundred dollars per day

---

[3] (At this level you are not even a blip on the casino's radar for casinos on the strip where table minimums are often $100).

times ten (10) days per month equal fifteen thousand dollars ($15,000) per month.

$125/roll X 2 rolls per shooter = $250 per shooter X 2 shooters per session = $500 per session X 3 sessions per day = $1,500 per day X 10 days per month = $15,000 per month.

You should **STOP** for the day if you lose more than $4,800 at any one session.*

*Lose $675 on PSO, double bet to $1,350. Lose again, double bet to $2,700. Lose again, STOP!!!! $675 + $1,350 + $2,700 = $4,725. If you want to be ultra conservative then do not double the bet. Keep it at $675 total combined bet. The reason being that it would only take an additional session (two shooters plus one additional roll) to make up for one loss.

At the end of month three you should have won another $15,000. **Add this to your initial bankroll. Do NOT spend it or use it for any other purpose!** Your bankroll should now be $36,800. ($5,000 + $3,000 + $3,000 + $5,400 + $5,400 + $15,000 = $36,800).

Repeat for months six and seven. If you remain at Level III your monthly income should be $15,000. This is equivalent to $180,000 per year. You can choose to play at a higher dollar amount if you want.

/ / / / /
/ / / / /
/ / / / /

LEVEL IV

Your Bankroll should be a minimum of $50,000 to with stand losses. Your Buy-in should be a minimum of $15,000 in case of a point Seven out or point number Seven out.

The bet is: One hundred dollars on the Four, Nine, Ten and Field; two hundred fifty dollars on the Five; and three hundred dollars on the Six and Eight each.

4	5	6	8	9	10	Field
$100	$250	$300	$300	$100	$100	$100 = $1,250

Bet just two (2) rolls per shooter **AFTER** the point is established. Based on the bet above you will win an average of two hundred fifty dollars ($250) per roll. Two hundred fifty dollars per roll time's two (2) rolls per shooter equal five hundred dollars ($500) per shooter. Five hundred dollars per shooter time's two (2) shooters per session equal one thousand dollars ($1,000) per session. One thousand dollars per session times three (3) sessions per day equal three thousand dollars ($3,000) per day. Three thousand dollars per day times ten (10) days per month equal thirty thousand dollars ($30,000) per month.

$250/roll X 2 rolls per shooter = $500 per shooter X 2 shooters per session = $1,000 per session X 3 sessions per day = $3,000 per day X 10 days per month = $30,000 per month.

You should **STOP** for the day if you lose more than $8,750 at any one session.*

---

*Lose $1,250 on PSO; (double bet) + $2,500 (lose again) + $5,000 (lose again) = $8,750 total loss. If you want to be ultra conservative then do not double the bet. Keep it at $1,250 total combined bet. The reason being that it would only take an additional session (two shooters plus one additional roll) to make up for one loss.

If you remain at Level IV your monthly income should be $30,000. This is equivalent to $360,000 per year.

"You must be locked in mentally to win. Be a Craps Robot!"

"If you do not see great riches in your imagination, you will never see them in your bank balance"
- Napoleon Hill

DISCLAIMER

The material contained in this book is intended to inform and educate the reader and in no way represents an inducement to gamble. *Gambling is extremely risky.* No guarantees or warranties are implied or expressed whatsoever. The reader assumes all responsibilities in implementing any betting strategy suggested or mentioned in this manual. Past performance is not indicative of future results. We strongly recommend that you read all the information that is available on the subject of craps from all authors, publishers, libraries and book stores. The information contained herein may have typographical errors or content errors.

Please use this book as intended and understand that neither the authors nor the publishers can accept responsibility or liability for any loss or damage attributed to the information and knowledge gained from reading the material provided in this book. **Each person must accept and assume all risk and liability from their actions.**

The strategies discussed in this manual have been tried and tested on actual craps tables in Las Vegas and Laughlin, Nevada; computer simulated craps, the automated craps game by *Organic* and against existing craps data bases. We do not recommend attempting to play any of the strategies discussed herein on an **on-line casino.**

This book is intended to be a teaching manual. In order to gain the most benefit from the information in these pages you must *read it over and over and over again; study*

it, and review it often. Take notes! If you don't understand something, look it up. Do not guess. Make sure you understand and comprehend what is being conveyed in this book. The story in this book is fiction. The information presented on how to win playing craps is real.

"If are not making money playing craps after reading this book, then you weren't paying attention."
- - David Medansky

A Word from the Authors:

While other books teach various betting strategies and money management, they only gloss over or superficially address walking away from the tables with a profit. **This book emphasizes the importance of setting specific, realistic and attainable goals along with the ability to walk away from the craps table with your profits. The most important lesson you can learn from reading this book is this: "It doesn't matter what method you use to win at the craps table; leave the table once you make your goal no matter how quickly you make it!"** It is not how much you win, but rather, how much of your winnings you keep. Some may refer to this as S.M.A.R.T. (Specific, Measurable, Attainable, Realistic and Timely) goals.

This book makes no assumptions about your knowledge of craps. Therefore, certain information will be discussed to help you be fully aware of and understand the craps layout, the types of bets that can be made and how to place bets. Information is provided so that you can be familiar and completely comfortable with craps jargon, lingo and terminology and know proper craps betting etiquette. Lastly, money management principles are discussed allowing you to determine what a sufficient bankroll is for the level of betting undertaken.

Recently, investing in the stock market has been compared to playing in a casino. Investment advisors get paid to assess risk properly. Similarly, in craps you win more consistently if you are able to assess risk properly. So, to be successful playing craps, you either need to be very lucky or you need to be able to minimize your risk. This book is based on analyzing the risk in each of the methods of betting/wagering at the craps table.

When people ask Medansky what he does for a living he

sometimes tells them he is in the risk management business.

A word about systems - It is extremely important to realize and to understand that no single betting method will consistently win. *There are no fool- proof strategies and there are no guarantees.* If someone is going to guarantee their betting strategy, we strongly encourage you not to walk away, but to run! Losses do and will occur. Each of the various methods taught by other authors will all work some of the time. None, in our opinion, will work all of the time. Is there more than one way to win at playing craps? Absolutely! As far as we are concerned, the only good bet is a winning bet. Likewise, the only bad bet is a losing bet. Nothing else really matters.

There is no such thing as a Holy Grail system. A Holy Grail is a system that allegedly works anytime, anywhere. Don't bother looking for it. It does not exist. **There is no single perfect system to play craps!** *Again, the purpose of this manual is to teach people basics of how the game of craps is played and various betting techniques that puts the player in the best possible position to win at the craps tables; and to set specific, measurable, attainable and realistic goals in a timely manner and to know when to walk away from the table. It is up to the individual person to maintain the discipline necessary to win.*

ARE YOU WILLING TO PUT IN THE TIME AND EFFORT TO LEARN THE GAME OF CRAPS? If not, then just play for the entertainment value. The chance of your winning consistently without any knowledge of the odds and the probabilities is exactly zero!

What we teach in this book is completely different from what most other experts and authors teach. That does not mean that what we teach is right and what others teach is wrong. It just means it is different. We shared with you what works for us. Whatever works for you - - great, keep doing it! Whatever doesn't work for you, toss out! Does that mean that everything we teach will work for you? Of course not! We shared with you what works for us and what works for others like Snake, "Little Joe," and S.A., who play and win on a regular and consistent basis. All we ask is that you keep an open mind. The strategies, philosophies, methodologies, and betting tactics discussed in this book are not theory or us saying they work; there are people right now implementing them and winning. Medansky's students have been shown these strategies in action and can attest to the reality of their success.

We suggest that you "Don't "believe" a word you read in this book." Why would we make such a statement? The reason is we are speaking from *our* experience; it does not make it right and it doesn't make it wrong. It doesn't make it true or false. We are simply sharing with you *our* experience. However, what we can tell you is that the information and strategies that you will learn in this book are based on countless hours on and off the tables of some of the greatest casinos around the world and these revelations have changed hundreds and hundreds and hundreds and hundreds of people's viewpoint of the game and how they play it!

APPENDIX A
THE BASIC GAME OF CRAPS

Craps is a relatively simple game. It is played with two dice. Each die has six sides numbered one through six. Thus, each cube has six equal possible outcomes when rolled. Casino dice are distinct, unlike dice used in other games such as Monopoly, Backgammon and other board games. Casino dice are larger with sharp pointed edges. Dice are transparent to prevent tampering by weighting each die (loaded dice). It is virtually impossible to weight the dice with a foreign material if you can see through the dice. Casino dice are also imprinted with the casino's logo or name and are coded with numbers so that a casino employee can verify their authenticity and prevent switching.

The individual rolling the dice is called the "shooter." The shooter must make either a Pass Line bet or a Don't Pass Line bet. The majority of the time, the shooter will make a Pass Line bet. Other players are also allowed to make a Pass Line bet. The shooter's first roll is called the "Come Out roll." If the Come Out roll is a 7 or 11, the shooter (and the other players), win their Pass Line bets. If the shooter rolls a 2, 3 or 12, (**2, 3 and 12 are craps numbers** - - this is where the name of the game is derived) the shooter and other players lose their Pass Line bets. If a number other than 2, 3, 7, 11 or 12, is rolled, that number becomes the shooter's point. The shooter must then roll that specific number before a 7 to win for the Pass Line bettors. If the shooter rolls a 7 before his point, the shooter loses for the Pass Line bettors and the dice are passed to the next player, who then becomes the shooter. The dice are passed around the table in a clockwise manner. Any other number is of no consequence. This is how craps has been played throughout history. This is also known as "street craps." Non-shooting players can bet with or against the shooter independently.

Casinos designed the craps layout to accommodate numerous types of bets. **Some of the available bets are not even shown on the layout**. Therefore, it is imperative that you learn as much about the possible types of bets that can be made as well as how those bets are paid.

In 1907, in New York City, a dice maker named John H. Winn introduced the first craps bank. With the craps bank, players bet against the bank, or the house, instead of each other. Winn charged both the Pass Line (right bettors, a player who believes the shooter will make his point before a seven) and the Don't Pass Line (wrong bettors, a player who believes the shooter will roll a seven before the point number) 25 cents (a quarter) for a $5 bet and 50 cents for a $10 bet. The 25 cent charge subsequently developed into a five percent charge. Because the five percent charge brought in so much money, so strongly and dependably, gamblers said it had "vigor." The gamblers took it one step further and changed the game's jargon by taking the word *vigor* and adding a syllable and called it *vigorish*. Later, some players shortened the word to *vig*. Throughout the years, **refinements have been made to the payouts by the house so that the edge is always with the house**. This edge for paying something other than true odds for the various bets is known as the ***"vig."***

"A dollar won is twice as sweet as a dollar earned." - - Paul Newman, *The Color of Money*

"The things that work best are always simple, because the more complicated a solution is the more chance it has to go wrong. Real success comes from putting all the small, simple things together into a system. If you faithfully do that, you will find yourself far ahead of the pack." - - Andrew Wood, *MAKING IT BIG IN AMERICA*

"Simplicity is the ultimate sophistication."
- Leonardo de Vinci

APPENDIX B
KEYS TO SUCCESS

The keys to success are: (1) have an adequate bankroll; (2) have a plan; (3) stick to your plan, i.e., maintain discipline; (4) exercise proper money management; (5) eliminate emotional errors; (5) some "good" luck and (6) *leave the table once you made your goal no matter how quickly or how you made it.* You must follow the proper protocol to be successful. Because craps is played at a fast pace, you must have a plan and know what you are going to do in advance. You must fend off any distractions or temptations that interrupt your plan. Stay focused on your goals and strategy no matter what is occurring at the table. Do not get caught up in other people's advice, criticism or betting strategies. Especially do not listen to dealers who may entice you to leave your bets on the table longer than you want or to make bets you would normally not make.

Remember, the dealers work for the casino. The dealer is not going to give you "good" advice to make money unless you are toking ("tipping") them. Keep in mind that if the dealer is so smart about making money playing craps then why is he or she dealing - - he or she would be playing professionally. Think about it. Have patience. Recognize that the majority of people who play craps lose.

Professional investors and money managers always have a plan for implementing their investment strategies. Professionals set realistic rates of returns (profits) for their investments before they make the investment and they limit losses with stop loss orders or know specific points at which to exit an investment if it does not perform as expected. In order to play craps to make money, you must set a realistic rate of return, how much you want to win before you make a bet. You must also know specifically when to stop if you are losing at a session and the betting strategy does not work as expected.

"There is a weird correlation between people who set goals and people who win." - - Dave Ramsey

MORE KEYS TO SUCCESS:

Winning is hard work - - there are no substitutes.
                                    – Dave Ramsey

To be successful playing craps, you must follow proper protocol. The most important element to be a successful craps player, as opposed to a lucky craps player, is to have and maintain DISCIPLINE!

- **SET GOALS**: Set specific realistic goals and draw downs (in event of a loss). I suggest your goal should be 20% of your buy-in. **Leave the table once you made your goal no matter how quickly or how you made it.**
- **PLAN**: Have a Plan of Action to achieve *your* goal.
- **BANKROLL**: Have an <u>adequate bankroll</u> to engage your plan. Never use more than 10% of your bankroll for a buy-in at any one session.
- **NEVER GAMBLE WITH MONEY YOU CANNOT AFFORD TO LOSE EITHER EMOTIONALLY OR FINANCIALLY. NEVER BORROW MONEY TO GAMBLE.**
- **KNOWLEDGE OF THE GAME**: Understand the bets you intend to make before you make the bet. Know the risk in making the bet before *you* make it.
- **BE FLEXIBLE: Be flexible with betting tactics based on what is happening at the table.**
- Stick to your plan; maintain <u>discipline.</u>
- **RISK MANAGEMENT**: Exercise proper money management.

- **LOSS EXIT POINT**: Have a pre-determined exit point if a losing session occurs, i.e., stop loss/limit loss. Losses do and will happen.
- Eliminate emotional errors.
- **FOCUS**: Stay <u>focused</u> on your goals and strategy no matter what else is going on at the table.
  - Fend off distractions or temptations that interrupt your plan.
  - Do not get caught up in other people's advice, suggestions, criticism or betting methods.
  - Never gamble when you are depressed, unhappy, tired or not feeling well.
  - Never drink alcohol or take drugs when playing craps.
  - Never increase your bets when you are losing.
- **CRAPS IS A BUSINESS**: Treat playing craps as a business.
- **HAVE PATIENCE**.
- Toke (tip) the dealers early and often. This keeps them engaged in the game, and they should help you if you forget to either make a bet or take down a bet.
- Keep an eye on your bets and make certain the dealer has made the proper bet for you. If you call your bets "off," make certain the dealer has placed the "Off" button to indicate so or takes your bets down. Make certain the dealer has paid you correctly.
- Know exactly what you are going to do *before* you walk into the casino and up to the craps table.
- **LUCK**: Some "good luck" also helps.

APPENDIX C
TYPES OF BETS

PASS LINE (sometimes referred to as Front Line): A "Pass Line" bet is made by placing a bet on the area of the table marked "Pass Line." The first roll of the dice by a new shooter is called the "Come-out roll." If the shooter's first roll of the dice is a 7 or 11 the Pass Line bettors win immediately. The Pass Line is paid even money. If the shooter's first roll of the dice is a 2, 3 or 12, ("craps") the Pass Line bettors lose immediately. The 2, 3, and 12 are called "craps" numbers. Hence the name of the game - - "Craps." Dealers will either pay you or take your money. If any number other than a 2, 3, 7, 11, or 12 is rolled by the shooter on the first roll of the dice (the "Come-out roll"), that number (4, 5, 6, 8, 9 or 10) establishes the shooter's point. These are sometimes referred to as "Box" numbers because the numbers are inside of a box on the layout.

Whenever a shooter establishes a point, the dealer will place a puck over that number on the table marking the point. Once a point is established, your Pass Line bet must remain on the table until the shooter either rolls the point number again (before a 7 is rolled), in which case you win, or rolls a 7 before the point number is rolled, in which case you lose. In any event, you cannot remove your Pass Line bet until you either win or lose. The Pass Line bet is considered to be a "*contract*" bet which means you either win or lose.

The shooter continues to roll the dice until he either makes his point or sevens-out. If the shooter makes his point, his next roll of the dice becomes a "Come-out roll." When the shooter sevens-out, the dice are offered to the next person on the shooter's left. The dice move around the table to the next shooter in a clockwise direction. A player has the option to "pass the dice" to the next player if he chooses not to roll the dice.

DON'T PASS LINE (DON'T PASS BAR) a/k/a "*The Dark Side*" (sometimes also referred to as the Back Line): A "Don't Pass Line" bet is made by placing a bet on the area of the table marked "Don't Pass" or Don't Pass Bar."

This bet is opposite of a Pass Line bet. If the shooter's first roll of the dice ("Come-out roll") is a 7 or 11, you immediately lose. If it is a 2 or 3, you immediately win the amount of your bet. The Don't Pass Line, as with the Pass Line bet, pays even money. If you bet $5, you will win $5. If the roll is a 12, it is called a push and you neither win nor lose. Any other number rolled: 4, 5, 6, 8, 9 or 10 becomes the shooter's point. If the shooter makes his point before a 7 is rolled, you lose. If a 7 is rolled before the point, you win. Unlike a Pass Line bet, a Don't Pass Line bet can be taken down (removed) at any time by the player. **A Don't Pass bet, however, cannot be made once a point is established by the shooter.** If the casino allowed you to make a Don't Pass bet *after* the shooter established a point, the advantage would be to the Don't Pass bettor (since there are more combinations for making a 7 than any other number) and the casinos would go broke.

COME BETS: A "Come" bet is made by placing a bet on the area of the table marked "COME." Come bets are even money bets with the same rules as a Pass Line bet, except when the puck used to mark the point is "Off," you cannot make a Come bet. This is because a shooter must establish a point for the Pass Line before a player can make a "Come" bet.

When you place your bet in the area on the table marked

"COME," the next roll of the dice acts just like a "Come-Out roll" for the Pass Line and will determine what happens to the Come bet. The first roll of the dice immediately after the bet is placed determines the "Come" point. If a 7 or an 11 are rolled, it is an automatic winner. If a 2, 3 or 12 are rolled it is an automatic loser. Any other number is called a point number for the person making the bet. The dealer moves the Come bet onto the number rolled inside of the "box."

For example, you put a $5 chip in the area marked "Come" on the layout. The shooter's next roll of the dice is a 6. The dealer will move your $5 chip to the inside of the box marked "Six." All Come bets are placed on the layout in relative position to where the player is standing. This bet pays even money. The bettor has the option to take odds on the "Come" bet, just like the Pass Line bet. Odds on the six pay 6 to 5. To make an "odds" bet on the "Come" bet you put your chips on the layout in the "Come" area and tell the dealer "$10 odds on the six. The dealer will then move your $10 odds bet and place it half-on, half-off on the $5 bet. Your $10 odds bet will pay you $12.

If the shooter rolls a 6 before a 7 you will be paid even money ($5) for your "Come" bet and $12 for your odds, a total of $17. The dealer will then stack your winnings with your bet and odds and set them in front of you on the table. If however, the shooter rolls a 7 before the "Come" point (6) you lose your bet. Any other number, i.e., 2, 3, 4, 5, 8, 9, 10, 11 or 12 will not affect the "Come" bet. It is considered a no-decision.

You could make a "Come" bet with every roll of the dice once a Pass Line point is established. This type of betting is *not recommended* because you will have too much money at risk if the shooter rolls a 7 before the shooter rolls the "Come" numbers. Often when a shooter sevens out and there is a "Come" bet you will hear the stick person say "seven out, line away, pay the don'ts, leave some for the Come."

DON'T COME BET *a/k/a "The Dark Side"* too: A "Don't Come" bet is betting the shooter will roll a 7 before the "Come Point" is rolled again. When the Puck used to mark the number is "OFF" you cannot make a Don't Come bet because *Don't Come Bets are placed only after a shooter establishes a point for the Pass Line.* Otherwise it is a Don't Pass bet. If you place a bet in the area of the table marked "**DON'T COME,**" the next roll of the dice acts like a "Come-Out" roll for the Pass Line.

What wins or loses when a bet is placed in the area of the table marked "DON'T COME" is opposite of what wins or loses for the Come bet. It is the same as the Don't Pass Line bet only it is *made* after the shooter establishes a Pass Line point. After you make a "Don't Come" bet, the first roll of the dice will determine the "Don't Come" point, unless a 7 or an 11 is rolled, in which case you lose, or a 2 or 3 is rolled, in which case you win, or a 12 is rolled, in which case, it is a "push" (neither win nor lose). Once a "Don't Come point is established (4, 5, 6, 8, 9 or 10), the only way your Don't Come bet will win is if a 7 is rolled before the "Don't Come" point. If the "Don't Come" point (4, 5, 6, 8, 9 or 10) is rolled again before a 7, you lose.

The dealer places a Don't Come bet in the small box *behind* the number indicating it is a "Don't Come" point. Hence the name "Back Line" is used for Don't Come bets. For example, the shooter has established a Pass Line point of 4. You decide to make a "Don't Come" bet and place $25 in the "Don't Come" box marked on the layout. The shooter rolls a 6 immediately after you placed your bet. The dealer will move your "Don't Come" bet to the small box behind the six. If a 6 is rolled again before a 7, you lose. If a 7 is rolled before a 6 is rolled again, you win. Many people will sometimes call "no action" (no bet) if a Don't Come point is a 6 or 8. This is because there are 6 ways to win if a 7 is rolled (1:6, 6:1, 2:5, 5:2, 3:4 and 4:3) and five ways to lose if a 6 or 8 is rolled (6 = 1:5, 5:1, 3:3, 2:4, 4:2 and 8 = 2:6, 6:2, 3:5, 5:3, 4:4). Other box numbers have lower possible combinations than the 7 and therefore a greater probability of winning. A player always has the option to take a Don't Pass or Don't Come bet down.

If you want to, you could make "Don't Come" bets with every roll of the dice after a point is established for the Pass Line. This type of betting is **not recommended** because you will have too much money at risk if the shooter rolls lots of numbers before a Seven.

PLACE BETS (sometimes referred to as "Box Numbers"): "Place bets" can be made at any time, even before a "Come-out roll." It is highly recommended that you wait to make a "Place" bet **after** the shooter establishes a point for the Pass Line. Place bets can only be made on the following numbers: 4, 5, 6, 8, 9, and 10. To make a "Place" bet you tell the dealer that you would like to place a bet on a specified number. The dealer puts your bet on the line of the "box" of the number that you want to bet on. If your Place number is rolled before a 7 is rolled, you win. If a 7 is rolled first, you lose. If other numbers are rolled it does not affect the Place bet.

A player cannot actually physically put chips on the layout for a "Place" bet. This is done by the dealer. The reason is that the "Place" bet area of the layout is similar to the dealer's cash register. The dealer physically puts the player's "Place" bets in certain areas based on where the player is positioned at the table. This enables the dealer to keep track of every player's money and "Place" bets when the table is busy. If players were allowed to physically put their "Place" bets on the layout it would create too much confusion and chaos. Other areas of the betting layout, such as Field bets, Pass Line and Don't Pass Line are considered "self-service" and are controlled by the player. *Never* attempt to place your chips on the Point Numbers area of the layout as this is done by the dealer. Again, to make a "Place" bet you tell the dealer on which numbers you want to make a bet and the dealer will physically put the chips indicating your bet on the layout. The box numbers area of the craps layout is analogous to a cash register. *Keep your hand out of the dealer's cash register!*

Place bets pay different odds depending on the number you bet on. For example, Four and Ten will pay 9 to 5 (bet $5 get paid $9), Five and Nine pay 7 to 5 (bet $5 get paid $7), and Six and Eight pay 7 to 6 (bet $6 to get paid $7). *Unlike a Pass Line bet, you have the option to call off or take down your Place bet anytime you want to do so.* Simply ask the dealer to take down your bets or tell the dealer your bets are not working. If the dealer does not take down your Place bets, make certain that he places a lamer, a button with the word "OFF" on your bets that indicates they are "OFF." Sometimes mistakes are made and you want to make certain that your bets are not working, that they are properly identified or marked as such.

FIELD BETS: To make a "Field" bet, place your wager in the area of the table marked **"FIELD."** It does not matter where in the Field you put your chips to make your bet because any

---

number rolled in the Field wins. **KEEP YOUR BETS DIRECTLY IN FRONT OF YOU** as much as possible. If you are standing in front of the "12" on the Field and you put your bet on the "3" or "4" (because they are your favorite numbers) the person standing in front of the "3" or "4" might think it is their bet and *take your chips if it is a winning roll.* This happens more often than people realize, especially at a crowded table. Field bets pay even money, unless a 2 or 12 are rolled. Depending on the casino, the 2 or 12 will pay double the bet; some may pay three times the bet. *The Field bet is a single roll wager.* If you place a bet in the area of the table marked "Field" and the next roll of the dice is a 2, 3, 4, 9, 10, 11, or 12 you win. If you forget to remove your winnings from the Field, it is considered a bet *("if it lays it plays").* If the next roll of the dice is a 5, 6, 7 or 8, you lose. Even though it may look like there are a lot of numbers on which you could win with a Field bet, it is sometimes referred to as a sucker bet. The reason being is that there are 20 ways to lose and only 16 ways to win. This is why understanding the probability of how often each number is likely to be rolled is so important.

An argument can be made that since the 5, 6, and 8 are lost on a 7 out, that the Field is not such a bad bet. If the 7 out is removed from the equation then there are 14 ways to lose on a Field bet and 16 ways to win. The fallacy with this thinking is that Field bets are a one roll bet - - win or lose. Whereas the 5, 6 or 8 remain regardless if a Field number is rolled. In addition, the 5, 6 and 8 pay more than even money, whereas the Field bet is paid even money, except if a 2 or 12 are rolled.

PROPOSITION BETS: To make a "Proposition" bet you toss your bet (chips) to the stickperson (the dealer who is calling the numbers and controlling the dice with the stick) at the center of the table and verbally state your bet. The stickperson will put your bet in the appropriate spot. Just as with Place bets, players are not allowed to physically put their proposition bets on the betting layout. The Proposition bets are a one roll of the dice bet with the exception of the Hard-way bets.

The layout for proposition bets can vary from one casino to another and from one table to another in the same casino. The Casinos use misdirection as to the correct payout to mislead players. There is a *distinction* between the meaning of the two little words "*to*" and "*for*". The way in which this deception operates can be shown as follows:

FOUR (4) THE HARD WAY AND TEN (10) THE HARD WAY: There are 3 ways to make either a 4 or 10 and 6 ways to make a 7. The player can only win one way for a Hard 4 (2:2) and only one way for a Hard 10 (5:5) and loses 8 ways (7 out, 3:1, 1:3 for the Hard 4 and 7 out, 6:4, 4:6 for the Hard 10). The correct odds should be 8 to 1. Most craps layouts will pay 7 to 1, thereby gaining an advantage. Many layouts will create the impression they are paying correct odds of 8 *to* 1 by indicating the payout is 8 *for* 1, meaning you are paid $7 plus your original $1 bet. Again, 8 *for* 1 is not the same as 8 *to* 1, wherein you are paid $8 plus your original $1. Some layouts will go even further to pay less for the hard way numbers by offering 7 *for* 1. As a further example, if you bet $5 on a Hard 4 and the shooter makes the Hard 4 (2:2), you will be paid $35 (7 x $5= $35). If you were paid the correct odds you should have been paid $40 (8 x $5 = $40). The same analysis applies to the Hard 10.

SIX (6) THE HARD WAY AND EIGHT (8) THE HARD WAY: There are 5 ways to make either a 6 or 8 and 6 ways to make a 7. The player can only win one way for a Hard 6 (3:3) and only one way for a Hard 8 (4:4) and loses 10 ways (7 out, 1:5, 5:1, 2:4 and 4:2 for the Hard 6 and 7 out, 2:6, 6:2, 3:5 and 5:3 for the Hard 8). The correct odds should be 10 to 1. Most craps layouts will create the impression they are paying correct odds of 10 *to* 1 by indicating pay 10 *for* 1, thereby gaining an advantage. Many layouts will indicate the payout is 9 *to* 1, meaning you are paid $9 plus your original $1 bet. Again, 10 *for* 1 is not the same as 10 *to* 1, wherein you are paid $9 plus your original $1. Some layouts will go even further to pay less for the hard way numbers by offering 9 *for* 1. As a further example, if you bet $5 on a Hard 6 and the shooter makes the Hard 6 (3:3), you will be paid $45 (9 x $5= $45). If you were paid the correct odds you should have been paid $50 (10 x $5 = $50). The same analysis applies to the Hard 8.

ANY CRAPS ("C"): If a 2, 3 or 12 ("craps") is rolled on the next roll of the dice, you get paid 8 for 1 (bet $1 gets paid $7 including your $1 for a total of $8). The "Any Craps" bets is only a one roll of the dice wager, win or lose.

Many players will use the Any Craps bet as a hedge on the Come-Out roll. For instance, if the player makes a Pass Line bet for $5, he may toss the dealer a $1 chip and say "Any Craps" or sometimes it is referred to as a "Crap Check" bet. If on the Come-Out roll a 2, 3 or 12 are rolled, you lose your $5 Pass Line bet but win $7 on your Any Craps bet, a net win of $2. If a 7 or 11 are rolled you win your $5 Pass Line bet, but lose your $1 Crap Check bet, a net win of $4. If any other number is rolled, which establishes the shooter's point, you lose your $1 Any Craps bet and the outcome of the Pass Line bet is determined by the shooter's roll.

You do not need to make a Pass Line bet to make an "Any Craps" bet. The "Any Craps" bet is a one roll bet that can be made anytime.

THREE WAY CRAPS: Sometimes when betting at higher levels, it is better to make a three way craps bet instead of an Any Craps bet. As an example, let's say you are betting $25 on the Pass Line. If you make a $3 Any Craps bet, you will be paid $21. If a craps number (2, 3 or 12) is rolled, you lose your $25 Pass Line bet but win $21 for your Any Craps bets, a net loss of $4.

If, however, you make a three way craps bet, you are in essence betting $1 on the 2 (1:1), $1 on the 12 (6:6) and $1 on the 3 (1:2 or 2:1). The $1 bet on the 2 (1:1) and 12 (6:6) will each pay $29, if it is rolled, resulting in a net win of $4 instead of a loss. However, if a 3 (1:2 or 2:1) is rolled you will only be paid $14, resulting in net loss of $11 because you lose your Pass Line bet.

One way to solve the discrepancy in the payouts is to also bet $1 on the ace-deuce (1:2) which will also pay $15. So your total hedge (insurance) bet is $4. Some players never want to hedge their Pass Line bet. Our recommendation is to always hedge a $25 (or higher) Pass Line bet, even if it is only a partial hedge. The choice is yours as to hedge the Pass Line bet or not.

ELEVEN ("YO") OR ("E"): If an 11 is rolled on the next roll of the dice, you get paid $15 plus your $1 is returned to you (bet $1 get paid $15). The Eleven, sometimes referred to as "Yo" or "E" is a one roll of the dice wager, win or lose.

The reason an eleven is referred to as "Yo" is to avoid confusion because *"seven"* sounds so similar to *"eleven."* The stick person wants to ensure that when he calls the number that there is no misunderstanding. So instead of just calling out "eleven" and someone thinking he said "seven" he adds "Yo" in front of eleven and calls out "Yo eleven." This is the same reason the numbers 6 and 9 are spelled out and appear on the layout as *"six"* and *"nine."* The dealer is looking at the numbers upside down so it is easy to get confused.

THE C-E BET: The "Craps-Eleven" bet, also known as "C & E" bet, is a wager that a 2, 3, 11, or 12 will be rolled on the next roll of the dice. It is only a one roll of the dice wager. If a 2, 3, or 12 are rolled, which is craps, the bet is paid 3 to 1. If an 11 is rolled, the bet is paid 7 to 1. C & E bets are placed by the stickperson in the small circles on either side of the Proposition bets in the center of the table. As an example, if you make a $5 "C" & "E" bet and a 2, 3, or 12 (craps) is the next roll, you will be paid $15 (3 X $5 bet = $15). If the shooter's next roll after the bet is an 11 instead of a 2, 3, or 12, you will be paid $35 (7 X $5 bet = $35). If any other number is rolled, you lose your $5 "C" & "E" bet. This bet can be made at any time.

HOP BET: Betting on the "Hop" means that you are betting that a specific number combination will be rolled on the very next roll. It is a one-roll wager. ***Many layouts do not show a hop bet on the felt.*** Still, the bet can be made. A player simply calls out *"$5 hopping the three-two"* and tosses a $5 chip to the stickperson. This means that the player expects the shooter to roll a 5 (3-2) on the very next roll of the dice. If the shooter rolls a 3-2 on the very next roll, he wins, if any other combination is rolled, the player loses. A Hop bet will pay 15 to 1, except a hard way (2:2, 3:3, 4:4, 5:5) hop which pays 30 to 1. Since it is a one-roll bet, and there is only one way to make that number out of 36 possible combinations, the casino pays 30 to one. For example, if a player calls out $1 hopping the hard eight, the shooter must roll a 4-4 on the very next roll of the dice for the player to win $30. If any other number is rolled, the Hard 8 Hop bet losses, whereas a regular Hard 8 bet will stay up (unless of course a 7 or easy 8 is rolled).

ANY SEVEN ("Big Red"): To make an "any 7" (also called a "Big Red" bet) simply toss your bet to the stickperson and call out the amount on "Any Seven" or "Big Red." If you toss a $1 chip to the stickperson and tell him $1 "Any 7" and a 7 is rolled on the very next roll of the dice, you get paid $4 plus your initial $1 bet (bet $1 to get paid $4). The Any Seven bet is only a one roll of the dice wager, win or lose and can be made anytime, even on the Come-out roll.

THREE WAY 7 BET HOPPING: The three way 7 hopping bet is only a one roll of the dice wager, win or lose and can be made anytime, even on the Come-Out roll. To make a three (3) way 7 hopping bet (this is slightly different than the Any Seven bet), you toss your bet in increments of 3 to the dealer and say "three way seven hopping." For example, you want to bet the three different combinations (2-5, 3-4, or 6-1) to make a 7. If any combination of 7 is rolled you are paid $15 to 1 at some casinos for a net win of $13 ($15 won, less the $2 loss on the other combinations of the 7). If you had made a $3 bet on the Any Seven, you would have won $12. So by betting $3 on a 3 way 7 *hopping* instead of $3 on an Any Seven, you would win $1 more. If you are making small size bets it does not seem like much, but with larger bet sizes it makes a huge difference. Sometimes it can be the difference between actually winning money and losing money.

Some players who do not bet on the Pass Line but want to participate on the Come-out roll will make a "Three Way 7 Hopping" bet, a "Yo - eleven" bet and an "Any Craps" bet. As an example, on the Come-out roll a player will toss the stickperson $3 and call out "Three Way 7 Hopping" and also toss the stickperson $1 for Any Craps and a $1 Yo for the eleven. These are just some of the little nuances of the game not taught in many books.

HARD WAY: Hard way bets are made if a 4, 6, 8 or 10 are made with a pair. In other words, a hard 4 can only be made with each dice being 2 (2 + 2 = 4), the hard six can only be made with each dice being 3 (3 + 3 = 6), the hard 8 can only be made with each dice being 4 (4 + 4 = 8), and the hard 10 can only be made with each dice being 5 (5 + 5 = 10). There is only one way and one way only to make each of the hard way numbers. *The hard way bets remain on the table for more than one roll of the dice.* You lose your hard way bet if the number (4, 6, 8 or 10) is made with any other combination of the dice or a 7. For example, if you bet $5 on the hard 6 and a 5 and 1 or a 2 and 4 is rolled before a 3 and 3, you lose. Of course, if a 7 is rolled before the 3 and 3 combination you also lose.

The probability of making the hard way numbers is less than other wagers and therefore you are paid more money if the hard way bet is made. The Four and Ten hard way will pay $8 for 1 (bet $1 get paid $7 plus your original $1); the Six and Eight hard way will pay $10 for $1 (bet $1 get paid $9 plus your original $1 bet). The reason the Hard Six and Hard 8 pay more than the Hard 4 and hard 10 is because there are more "easy" combinations to make a six or 8, than the 4 or 10, thus more ways to lose.

To make a hard way bet simply toss your bet to the stickperson and call out your bet. For instance, if you are betting $5 on all of the hard way numbers you toss $20 ($5 for each number) to the stickperson and say "all of the hard ways please." The stickperson will then place your wager in the appropriate spot on the layout indicating your bet.

Another thing to know about the hard way bet is that on a Come-out roll they are working unless called off.[4] What this means is that if the shooter has made his point and there is a new come out roll, your hard way bets are still working unless you call them off. If the shooter rolls a 7 on the come out roll, you lose your hard way bets. If your bets are "off" you do not lose. By the same token, if your bets are "off" and a hard way number is rolled you do not win. Many people like to turn their hard way bets off because Pass Line bettors want a 7 to appear on the come out roll. The stick person will call out "Hard ways work unless called off" or something to that effect. These bets stay on the layout through several Come-out rolls using "Off" and "On" designations.

Another interesting fact about a hard way bet is that if you hop a hard way (remember a hop bet is a one roll bet win or lose) you will be paid 30 to 1 instead of the normal 7 to 1 for the 4 and 10 hard way or 9 to 1 for the 6 and 8 hard way.

BIG 6 AND BIG 8: At the corners of the craps layout are two boxes marked with the large figures 6 and 8. This is the area for placing a bet on the "Big 6" and "Big 8." "Big 6" and "Big 8"

---

[4] "Hardways working on the Come-out roll may vary from casino to another.

bets are wagers that a 6 or an 8 will be rolled before a 7. These bets pay even money as opposed to Place bets on the 6 or 8 which pay 7 to 6. Clearly, if you were going to make a bet on the 6 or the 8 you would not make a bet on the "Big 6" or "Big 8" since you would win more with a place bet on the 6 and 8. Because these bets are rarely made anymore, many "newer" craps layouts no longer show the "Big 6" and "Big 8."

ACE-DEUCE: If ace-deuce (1:2) is rolled on the next roll of the dice, you get paid 15 to 1 (bet $1get paid $15 plus your $1 bet). The Ace-Deuce bet is only a one roll of the dice wager, win or lose.

SNAKE EYES ("2") AND BOX CARS ("12"): "Snake Eyes" ("aces on the faces") is a bet where a pair of 1's is thrown on the very next roll of the dice. Similarly, "Box Cars" ("midnight") is a bet where a pair of 6's is thrown on the very next roll of the dice. The payout is 30 for 1, (for every bet $1 on each, get paid $29 plus your original $1 bet). Some people will bet both "Snake Eyes" and "Box Cars" which is sometimes referred to as a "High/Low" bet.   If you make a "High/Low" bet instead of individual bets on the 2 and 12, the payout is 15 for 1.

HORN BET: The "Horn" bet is another bet that sometimes does not have a designated area marked on the layout of the craps table. A Horn bet is a wager that a 2, 3, 11 or 12 will appear on the next roll of the dice. The difference between a Horn bet and a C & E bet is that the Horn bet is actually four separate bets, in that you are placing one bet on four numbers. This means that the minimum Horn bet is four times what each bet would be. As an example, suppose you want to bet the Horn, you would need to bet $4 (one dollar each for the 2, 3, 11 and 12). If the shooter rolls either a 2 or a 12, you are paid $26 plus your $4 original bet remains up unless you call it down. If a 3 or 11 is rolled, you are paid $11 plus your original $4 bet remains up, unless called down. If any other number is rolled, you lose your Horn bet.

The Horn bet is only a one roll of the dice wager, win or lose and can be made anytime, even on the Come-out roll.

THE WORLD (or "Whirl"): the "World" bet is a Horn bet which also includes the Any Seven. In other words, the World bet is a bet which includes the numbers 2, 3, 11, 12 and 7. To make a World bet simply toss the stick person a $5 chip and ask the stick person for a World bet. The $5 represents $1 bet on the 2, 3, 11, and 12 each, a total of $4 and $1 on the 7 (Big Red). In essence, if a 7 is rolled by the shooter it covers the World bet. If the shooter rolls either a 2 or a 12, you are paid $25 plus your $5 original bet remains up unless you call it down. If a 3 or 11 are rolled, you are paid $10 plus your original $5 bet remains up, unless called down. If any other number is rolled, you lose your World bet. The World bet is only a one roll of the dice wager, win or lose and can be made anytime, even on the Come-out roll.

PLACING OR LAYING ODDS: Odds bets, also known as "Free Odds," are so named because the house has no advantage over the player. *The Free Odds bet is not marked anywhere on the layout of the craps table.* Sometimes it is referred to as "Behind the Line" odds. The Free Odds bet is the most important wager that a player can make playing craps the "conventional" way. To make an odds bet, the player must either make a Pass Line bet, Come bet, Don't Pass Line bet, or Don't Come bet. In other words, the Free Odds bet is not an independent bet which can be made. It can only be made in conjunction with another bet.

When you place an Odds bet with either the Pass Line or Come bet, you are "taking" the odds. When you are putting odds behind the Don't Pass Line or Don't Come bet, you are "laying" the odds.

Free Odds pay according to the probability for the specific point to be rolled. The 4 or 10 pay two to one (there are 3 ways to make either a 4 or 10 and 6 ways to lose on a 7, hence $6 \div 3 = 2$ to 1); the 5 or 9 pay three to two (there are four ways to make either a 5 or 9 and 6 ways to lose on a 7, hence $6 \div 4 = 3$ to 2); and the six and eight pay six to five (there are 5 ways to make either a 6 or 8 and 6 ways to lose on a 7, hence $6 \div 5 = 6$ to 5). For example, a $5 odds bet on the 4 or 10 pays $10; and a $5 odds bet on the 6 or 8 pays $6. Since the 5 and 9 pay three to two, casinos usually require you bet even amounts for free odds. So if the point is 5 or 9 and you take free odds you bet $6. The $6 bet will pay $9. If you were to bet $5 as free odds on the 5 or 9 the payout would be $7.50. But since casinos for the most part do not use 50¢ chips, they would only pay you $7.

ODDS – PASS LINE AND COME BET

Once a point is established, the Pass Line bettor can take an amount of chips in equal value to the original Pass Line bet (except if the point is 5 or 9 as noted above) and place these chips (your odds bet) directly behind your Pass Line bet. You will now have on the layout a wager on the Pass Line and a wager behind the line (free odds bet). If the shooter makes his point, you will be paid even money on your Pass Line bet and more than even money on your free odds bet. The exact payout on your free odds bet depends on the shooter's point number (4 & 10 pay 2 to 1; 5 & 9 pay 3 to 2 and 6 & 8 pay 6 to 5).

For example, let's say you make a $5 Pass Line bet. The shooter establishes the 4 as his point number. You take odds behind the line in the amount of $5. Most casinos will let you take double odds or more. "Double Odds" means that you can bet twice the amount of your Pass Line bet for an odds bet. The person next to you also makes a $5 Pass Line bet, but he takes double odds and puts $10 behind the line. The shooter makes his point of 4. You are paid $5 for your Pass Line Bet and $10 for your $5 odds bet, a total of $15. The person next to you is paid $5 for his Pass Line Bet and $20 for his $10 odds bet, a total of $25.

Free odds can also be made on all Come bets just the same as on the Pass Line bet. Remember, a Come bet can only be made after the shooter establishes a point.

Free odds may be removed or reduced at any time by a player. Since they work in favor of the player, many experts recommend they should never be taken down. Also, odds are *NEVER* working on a Come-out roll. As an example, let's say that during the shooter's roll you established two other numbers, the 6 and 9 as Come bets. You gave the dealer the proper amount for odds. The shooter makes his point and is now establishing a new point on the Come-out roll. If the shooter rolls a 7, you lose your Come bets on the 6 and 9, but the dealer will return your odds to you. By the same token, if the shooter rolls a 9 on the Come out roll, the dealer will only pay you for your Come bet without paying the odds. The dealer will simply return your odds to you.

As an example, you have a $5 come bet on the 9 with $6 odds. If the shooter rolls a 7 on the Come-out roll, you lose your

$5, but the dealer returns your $6 odds bet. But, if the shooter rolls a 9 on the Come-out roll to establish his new point, the dealer will pay you $5 for your come bet and return your odds without paying you. Taking it one step further, if the shooter establishes a new point of 8 and you have a $5 come bet on the 9 with $6 odds and the shooter rolls a 9, the dealer will pay you $5 for your Come bet and $9 for your $6 odds bet, a total of $14, plus return your original bets. Although this may sound confusing, once you practice and understand it, it becomes rather simple.

ODDS – DON'T PASS LINE AND DON'T COME BETS:
Once a point is established, you are permitted to make a free odds bet on the Don't Pass Line. Since the odds favor the Don't Pass Line bettor once the point is established, (there are more ways to roll a 7 than any point number), and the Don't Pass bettor must *lay* odds. This is where the bettor will put up more money on the Free Odds bet than he will win. In other words, you are betting as if you are the house. The odds on the Don't Pass Line bet are exactly opposite of the Free Odds bets made for a Pass Line bet. For example, if the point is 4 or 10, you will need to lay $10 for Free Odds to make $5 (betting 2 to make 1); if the point is 6 or 8, you will need to lay $6 for Free Odds to make $5 (betting 6 to make 5); and if the point is 5 or 9, you will need to lay $9 for Free Odds to make $6 (betting 3 to make 2).

Free Odds bets can also be made on all Don't Come bets at the same odds as on the Don't Pass Line bet. A Don't Come bet is the same as a Don't Pass Line bet, except it is made after the point is already established.

Free Odds bets on the Don't Pass Line or Don't Come

may be removed or reduced at any time by the player. These are the bettor's best bet since there are more ways to roll a 7 than any other point number. Removing the odds on a Don't bet should not be done - - unless there is a "hot" shooter or a dice influencer who is the shooter. This will be explained later.

BUYING THE 4, 5, 6, 8, 9 OR 10. The casino gives the player an option to "buy" a place number for a five percent commission on your bet. To "buy" a place number, you must pay the casino a 5% commission on your bet. Once you have bought a number, the casino will pay-off your bet at the correct or true odds. Thus, for a bet on the 4 or 10, the pay-off will be two to one rather than nine to five as is the usual pay-off for these bets. Most people do not buy the 5, 6, 8, or 9 because the difference in the pay-off for the correct odds is not significant enough. Thus, you will mostly see people "buying" the 4 or 10.

APPENDIX D
GLOSSARY OF CRAPS JARGON

ACE-DEUCE: A term for the number 3 on a pair of dice, i.e., 2:1 or 1:2.

ACE: The one spot or pip on a die (single dice).

ACTION: Betting, wagering or bets.

ADA FROM DECATUR: Slang expression for the number 8 in craps.

ANTI-MARTINGALE: The opposite of the *Martingale* system in gaming. This involves doubling the bet size after winning, as opposed to doubling the bet after a loss.

ANY CRAPS: A one roll wager that the next roll of the dice will be a 2, 3, or 12. The payout is 8 for 1 or 7 to 1. Bet $1, get paid $7 plus your original bet for a total of $8.

ANY SEVEN: A one roll wager that the next roll of the dice will be a 7 (1:6, 2:5, or 3:4).

BACK LINE: Is a term for the Don't Pass betting area of a craps layout, or, referring to that type of betting activity.

BANK CRAPS: The game of craps wherein players bet against the house instead of each other. Sometimes bank craps is referred to as casino craps as opposed to street craps.

BANKROLL: The amount of money a person sets aside specifically for the purpose of playing craps, or for placing bets on any other types of games of chance.

BAR: A come-out roll of 12 is a tie on the Don't Pass Line. You do not win, you do not lose. It also applies to Don't Come bets.

BAREBACK: Placing a bet without a hedge bet as protection against losing to a long shot. This term generally applies to situations involving large, odds-on wagers.

BET: An amount of money used for speculative investment at a game of chance. This is also referred to as a wager.

BET THE DICE TO WIN: Making a bet on the Pass Line.

BEHIND THE LINE: A bet on the free odds after a point has been established on the come-out roll.

BELLY UP: To lose all of your money; to go broke.

BETTING RIGHT: Betting the Pass Line or Come area of the table layout.

BETTING WRONG: Betting the Don't Pass Line or Don't Come area of the table layout.

BETTOR: A person who places wagers or makes bets.

BIG DICK: A slang expression for the number 10.

BIG SIX AND BIG EIGHT: An even money bet that the six or eight, whichever is the bet, will be rolled before a 7 is rolled. Many table layouts no longer have this bet marked because it is not a good bet for the player and many people were ignoring these bets.

BLACK CHIPS: $100 chips.

BOX CARS: Is a pair of sixes on the dice; 12.

BOXMAN/BOXPERSON: A casino employee who supervises and oversees the craps table from a seat between the two dealers opposite of the stickperson.

BOX NUMBERS: The boxes numbered 4, 5, 6, 8, 9 & 10 which are used to mark the shooter's point and to mark Place, Come and Buy bets.

BUY THE 4 OR 10: Paying a 5% commission to the casino in order to be paid correct (true) odds of 2 to 1 on the bets made on the 4 or 10. It is an alternative to a place bet on the 4 or 10 which pays 9 to 5 instead of 2 to 1.

BUCK: Another term for the marker (looks like a hockey puck) used to indicate or mark the shooter's point.

BUY-IN: The cash exchanged for chips (checks) at the beginning of table wagering. As an example, a person walks up to a craps table and sets down a $100 bill and asks for change. The dealer will give him $100 in chips. The $100 is considered to be the persons buy-in.

CASHIER: One who handles monetary transactions in a casino. This includes exchanging gaming tokens or cheques for cash, or processing payments for cash advances or markers.

CENTER BETS: Same as Proposition bets.

CHANGE COLOR/COLOR UP: To change checks (chips) from lower to higher denominations and vice versa.

CHEQUE: A casino gaming chip or token used as money in a casino.

CHICKEN FEEDER ("CF"): Slang term used to describe a shooter that rolls or tosses the dice hap hazard as if feeding chickens.

CHIP: A gaming token used as money in a casino. It is synonymous with "check."

COLD DICE OR COLD TABLE: A table where Pass Line bettors are losing and Don't Pass Line bettors are winning. It is also a term for a table where shooters are sevening out early during their roll.

COLOR OUT: A term used by a player to inform the dealers that they are leaving the table and wish to convert their gaming chips to higher denominations.

COME BET: A bet made after a point has been established by the shooter on a come-out roll. A come bet is the same as a Pass Line bet, but is made only after the shooter has established a point. Come bets are automatic winners if a 7 or 11 is rolled; automatic losers if a 2, 3, or 12 is rolled. Any other number becomes the point number for the come bet and must be made again before a 7 is rolled to win. If a seven (7) appears before the Come Number, the bet is lost.

COME-OUT ROLL: The roll made by a shooter before any point has been established.

COMP: Free goods and services, i.e. free rooms, meals, shows, etc. given to players by the casino in exchange for their action.

CRAPS: The term to describe when a shooter rolls a 2, 3, or 12. Craps numbers are automatic losers for Pass Line bettors on a Come-out roll or a Come bet.

CRAP OUT: When a shooter rolls a 2, 3 or 12 on the Come-out roll.

CREW: The four casino personnel who staff the craps table at the casino.

CROOKED DICE: Dice that have been tampered with so as not to give a random roll.

DARK SIDE: A player betting on the Don't side, either the Don't Pass Line or the Don't Come or both.

DEALER: The name for any casino employee who works at a craps table.

DEUCE: The number 2 on a die, not to be confused with two 1's which equals 2 and is referred to as "snake-eyes."

DICE: A pair of six-sided cubes marked on all sides with dots or "pips" denoting the numbers used at craps and other games. Generally casino dice are referred to as precision dice because they have extremely sharp edges and are made with a small tolerance for variances.

DICE FIXING: Sometimes referred to as dice setting where a shooter sets the dice in a certain position prior to the roll to influence the outcome.

DIE: Singular for dice, one of the six sided cubes used to play craps.

DON'T COME BET: A bet made in the area of the craps table marked "Don't Come." A bet made after the shooter has established a point that the next number established by the shooter will lose. It is the opposite of a Come bet.

DON'T PASS LINE BET: A bet made on the Come-out roll that the dice will not repeat the point number established by the shooter before a 7 is rolled. It is an automatic winner if the number rolled on the Come-out is 2 or 3; automatic loser if the number is 7 or 11; and a tie if a 12 is rolled.

DOUBLE ODDS BET: A free odds bet at double the Pass Line bet.

EASY, EASY WAY: The roll of a 4, 6, 8 or 10 where the dice are not matched as a pair, such as 3-3, 4-4, 5-5 or 2-2 (Hard way), but in other combinations such as 3-1, 5-3, 6-2, etc.

EDGE: The advantage either the casino or a player has on a particular wager. An edge is usually expressed as a percentage.

EVEN MONEY: A wager that is paid off at $1 for a $1 bet.

FIELD BET: A bet placed in the area of the craps layout marked "Field" that the next roll of the dice will be any of the following numbers: 2, 3, 4, 9, 10, 11 or 12. The wager pays even money unless a 2 or 12 is rolled which pays 2 to 1 or sometimes 3 to 1 depending on the casino.

FIXING THE DICE: This is a term used to describe the art of a shooter setting the dice so as to influence the outcome of the dice.

FLAT BET: Always betting the same amount of money.

FLOORMAN/FLOOR PERSON: A casino employee who supervises one or more craps tables.

FREE ODDS: An extra bet made behind the Pass Line, Come bet, Don't Pass Line or Don't Come bet after the point has been established, that is paid off at true odds.

FRONT LINE: Another name for the Pass Line bet.

GAMBLER: A person who puts money at risk for speculative gain as a profession.

GAMING: This is another term used by the casinos to describe gambling. Casinos refer to gambling as the gaming industry. In gambling, a person is betting a little money to make a lot of money with a high probability of losing, i.e., playing the lottery. In gaming, the casinos are putting up a large amount of money to make a little bit of money but with a high probability of winning. For example, slot machines pay out 98%. What this actually means is that the casinos are making 2% on every dollar bet. They win no matter what happens.

GAMBLING STAKE: A specific amount of money set aside for gambling purposes.

GEORGE: A player who tips the dealers regularly.

GIRL'S BEST FRIEND: Slang for the hard ten bet.

GREEN: $25 chips. Green chips are also referred to as quarters.

HARD WAY BETS: A bet made in the center of the table that the numbers 4, 6, 8, or 10 will be made as 2-2, 3-3, 4-4, or 5-5 respectively before they are made "easy" or a 7 is rolled.

HIGH ROLLER: An individual who wagers large sums of money at the craps table or any other table game.

HOP BET: A bet that on the very next roll of the dice a specific number combination will appear such as *"2 and 3 on the hop"*, which means a 2 and a 3 totaling 5 will appear. Hop bets are paid 15 to 1 and are usually only available in Nevada casinos. In addition, hop bets are generally not marked or indicated on the craps table layout.

HORN BET: A one roll proposition bet that on the very next roll of the dice a 2, 3, 11, or 12 will be rolled. Since the bet covers four numbers, it requires four betting units. If you want to make a horn bet, you will usually need to bet a minimum of $4 ($1 for each of the numbers). Many times bettors will make a $20 Horn bet ($5 on each number). The pay out for a "2" or "12" is 30 to 1 and the payout for a "3" or "11" is 15 to 1.

HOT ROLL: Numerous rolls of the dice where numbers other than a 7 are thrown by the shooter for an extended period of time. A winning table for players betting that the dice will pass, i.e., the point number is made by the shooter several times.

HOUSE: A casino, the entity a player bets against.

HOUSE ADVANTAGE: The term "house advantage" refers to the statistical advantage in favor of the casino, derived by paying off winning bets at a rate below the true odds. This is also referred to as vigorish or the vig.

INSIDE NUMBERS: The place numbers 5, 6, 8 and 9.

JUNKET: An organized group of players who are treated to either free trips to the casino or are given rooms and food below market value in return for the player spending time gambling at the casino.

LAYOUT: The felt surface of the craps table where all bets are placed, paid off, collected, and where the dice are thrown.

LAY THE ODDS: An odds bet by a player betting against the number, i.e., betting that the 7 appears before the number; a *"free odds"* bet made as a supplement to the *"don't pass"* bet.

LINE BET: Refers to a bet made on either the Pass Line or the Don't Pass Line.

LAY WAGER: A place bet made by a don't bettor who pays a 5% commission to the casino for making such a bet.

LIMITS: The maximum and minimum size bets allowed at the craps tables.

LITTLE JOE: A slang term for the number 4.

LOADED DICE: Dice that have been weighted to alter their roll are referred to as loaded.

LOSS LIMIT: A monetary amount or margin applied to a bankroll which is not to be exceeded. This is designed to protect the player from making foolish bets. An amount of money a bettor will not exceed if losing.

LUMPY: A dealer who often makes mistakes.

MARKER: An IOU signed by a player with established credit at a casino.

MARTINGALE: A system which involves doubling one's bet size after each loss as often as necessary in an effort to recover prior losses.

MIDNIGHT: A craps slang term for a dice roll of 12.

MINI-MARTINGALE: A variation to the martingale system wherein a player stops the series of doubling his bets and accepts the loss if a win is not produced within a certain number of bets.

MISS, MISS OUT: A term for a roll where a shooter sevens out.

NATURAL: A slang term for a 7 or 11 rolled on the come-out roll.

NICKELS: $5 chips.

NUMBERS: The numbers 4, 5, 6, 8, 9, or 10 called for by a player to be rolled by the shooter.

ODDS: The correct ratio or probability of determining whether or not an event will occur at the craps table or other casino games.

OFF ("TAKE MY BETS OFF!"): A verbal call made by the player instructing the dealer that his bet is not working (will not count) on the next roll of the dice. Bets that are "off" are inactive and are not subject to winning or losing.

ONE ROLL BET: A bet at the craps table determined by the very next roll of the dice that it will either win or lose. These are usually field bets, hop bets, or proposition bets.

ON: A craps bet that is working. A verbal instruction by a player to the dealer that his bet previously turned off is now active.

OSCAR'S GRIND: One of the more effective betting systems for even money bets known to gamblers to make money. See Chapter 10.

OUTSIDE NUMBERS: The place numbers 4, 5, 9 and 10 on the craps layout.

PARLAY OR PRESS: The act of betting your original bet plus all of the winnings forming a new, larger bet.

PASS: The point number being made.

PASS LINE: The area on the craps table where a Pass Line bet is made where players seek the repeat of the point number before a 7 is rolled.

PAYOFF, PAYOUT: The paying off of the winning bets by the casino.

PIT BOSS: A higher level casino executive in charge of supervising the gaming tables.

PLACE BETS: A bet on one of the point numbers 4, 5, 6, 8, 9 or 10 on the place box area of the craps table layout that the designated number will be rolled before a 7. The 4 & 10 pay $9 to $5; the 5 & 9 pay $7 to $5; and the 6 & 8 pay $7 to $6.

PLACE NUMBERS: One of the six point numbers: 4, 5, 6, 8, 9, or 10 on which a place bet is made at the craps table.

POINT: A point number (4, 5, 6, 8, 9 or 10) established by a shooter on the come out roll which must be made again before a 7 is rolled.

PRECISION SHOOTER: A player who consistently sets the dice the same way, always grips them the same way and always tosses them the same way in an effort to influence the outcome of the dice.

PRESSING A BET: To increase the size of the bet, usually by doubling it after a win.

PROGRESSION: A series of bets that increase in size until a win occurs, at which time a new series may begin.

PROPOSITION OR CENTER BETS: The bets located at the center of the craps table layout promoted by the stickperson.

PUCK: A disk used to mark the point established by the shooter on the come out roll. When the puck is "Off", the shooter is on a come out roll to establish a point. The puck will be on placed on the Don't Come area of the craps layout. When the puck is "On" the shooter has already established a point and the puck will be positioned on that number by the dealer.

PUSH: The term for a tie in gambling where the player does not lose his bet.

PUT BET: A Put bet is a late Pass Line bet (a Pass Line bet made after the Come-out roll and a point is already established).

QUARTERS: $25 casino chips, usually green in color.

RAILS: A term for the grooved area carved into the arm rest of the craps table where the player keeps his chips.

RATING: The casino's evaluation of a player's action to determine the level of comps.

REGRESSION: A term to describe a bet that is reduced in amount than the prior bet.

RIGHT BETTOR: A player who bets the Pass Line; or any other bet that is vulnerable to the 7.

ROLL OR THROW: An individual toss of the dice. The act of throwing the dice by the shooter.

SCARED MONEY: Money the player is afraid to lose. Money not specifically set aside for gambling.

SEVEN-OUT: The 7 being rolled after the shooter has established a point, but before the point number has been rolled. A seven out causes a loss for the Pass Line bettor and a win for the Don't Pass Line bettor.

SHILL: A person hired by the casino to play table games as a way to attract other players to the table.

SHOOT: All the rolls of a single shooter until he sevens out. A term used for a complete series of rolls by a shooter before he sevens out.

SHOOTER: The player rolling the dice.

SIC PARVIS MAGNA: Great things have small beginnings.

SILVER: $1 tokens or dollar chips.

SINGLES: The term for $1 gaming chips/checks.

SNAKE EYES: A slang term for the number 2 being rolled by the shooter; a pair of ones. Aces on the faces.

SOFT: Another term used for "easy" for the numbers 4, 6, 8 or 10.

STAKE: The bankroll used for gambling.

STANDOFF: A tie or "push."

STICKMAN/STICK-PERSON: The dealer who calls the game and handles the dice with a long hooked stick. He is also the person responsible for the center or proposition bets.

THREE-WAY CRAPS: A hedge bet that covers the three craps numbers of 2, 3 and 12 with three chips and pays relative to the odds for each of those numbers. Similar to a *horn* bet except the 11 is not covered.

TOKE: A tip for the dealers.

"TOO TALL TO CALL": An expression used by the dealer at a craps table when one or both of the dice has landed in the rail.

VIG: An abbreviation for *vigorish*.

VIGORISH: The casino's edge or advantage.

WAGER: A bet.

WALKING THE PLANK: A bet where you lay the 10 and after each roll move the bet to the next number, i.e., the 9, then the 8, the 6, etc in the hope of a 7 being rolled before a lay number.

WHALE: A big bettor. A *high roller* who bets large amounts of money.

WHITE: A $1 gaming chip. Some casinos use other colors to denote $1 chips so the term may not apply.

WORKING (MY BETS ARE WORKING."): A verbal call made by the player that his bets are active and that the bets count as to either winning or losing.

WORLD BET (Sometimes denoted as "Whirl" on the layout): A five-unit bet that combines the four parts of a *horn* bet with the *any seven* bet. The payoff is in accordance with the odds for each component.

WRONG BETTOR: A player who bets against the numbers and with the 7. A term used to describe a Don't Pass Line and Don't Come bettor. *See* Dark Side.

YO-ELEVEN: A slang term for the number 11. Yo bets are often made on the come-out roll.

The poker movie **Rounders** with Matt Damon and Edward Norton
has great advice **not** only for playing poker, but for playing craps.
Below is just some of that wisdom.

Matt Damon (Mike McDermott) narrating:
"Guys around here'll tell ya... *you play for a living.*
It's like any other job. You don't gamble. You grind it out.
Your goal is to win one big bet an hour, that's it.
Get your money in when you have the best of it, and protect it when
you don't. Don't give anything away." (Emphasis added).

"Don't got the stones? You ignorant punk. I play for money. I owe
rent. Child support. I play for money, not the fuckin' world series of
ESPN." (Emphasis added) - - Joey Knish

"It hurts doesn't it? Your hopes dashed your dreams down the
toilet. And your fate is sitting right besides you." - - Teddy
KGB

(This is how I have felt many times after doubling my
bet only to have a seven out be the next roll of the dice.)

I've often seen these people, these squares at the table, short stack
and long odds against them. All their outs gone. One last card in
the deck that can help them. I used to wonder how they could let
themselves get into such bad shape, and how the hell they thought
they could turn it around. - - Mike McDermott (Matt Damon)

"Mike, I learned it from you. You always told me this was the rule.
Rule number one: Throw away your cards the moment you know
they can't win. Fold the fucking hand." - - Joey Knish

You can shear a sheep many times, but skin him only once.
- - Mike McDermott [*quoting a gambling maxim*]

If you do not fully grasp the concepts or the wisdom of the quotes
above you have missed the entire point for us writing this book.

Thank you for purchasing

Greatest Craps Guru.

If you like our novel, please

write a review on

Amazon.com

And Goodreads.com

Thank you for your support!

Other Books by David Medansky

Flamingo's Baby – A Novel

Wholly Craps – A Teaching Manual

Walk Away Craps

Craps: A Winning Strategy

You can contact the authors at greatestcrapsguru@gmail.com.

David Medansky can also be reached at 602-721-5218.

My good friend, David Medansky and his friend former Denver Broncos football player Mark Jackson, have written a new book called "The Greatest Craps Guru". I have read the book and I give the book a BIG THUMBS UP !!! The story is a fictional story about a professional craps player and a professional football player and how the craps player tries to instill his craps playing insight to the football player. Much of the information in the book was not new to me, but reading the book and reading the insights shared in the book helped to center and ground MY PERSONAL craps game. I can be kind of stubborn when it comes to people telling me, teaching me, or selling me something new when it pertains to the game of craps - but I would STRONGLY recommend this book to improve your craps game. This book caused me to re-evaluate what I was doing at the craps table and get back to the basics that I had done years ago. I have not had a losing session since I have read the book and re-evaluated my craps game! I strong encourage you to take advantage of the information and insight in this book!!!

                                    - Snake of *Little Joe Craps*

Made in the USA
Lexington, KY
30 September 2015